MAPPING THE FIELD OF ADULT AND CONTINUING EDUCATION

Volume One

MAPPING THE FIELD OF ADULT AND CONTINUING EDUCATION

An International Compendium

VOLUME ONE: Adult Learners

EDITED BY

Alan B. Knox, Simone C. O. Conceição, and *Larry G. Martin*

Consulting Editors: Lisa M. Baumgartner, Michelle Glowacki-Dudka, Mark Tennant, and Allan Quigley

Editorial Coordinator: Anita Samuel

Foreword by Steven B. Frye

Co-published with

Stylus
STERLING, VIRGINIA

Published by Stylus Publishing, LLC.
22883 Quicksilver Drive Sterling,
Virginia 20166-2102

Library of Congress Cataloging-in-Publication Data
Names: Knox, Alan B. (Alan Boyd), 1931- editor. |
Conceição, Simone C. O., 1963- editor. |
Martin, Larry G., editor.
Title: Mapping the field of adult and continuing education : an international compendium / edited by Alan B. Knox, Simone C.O. Conceição, and Larry G. Martin ; editorial coordinator Anita Samuel.
Description: First edition. |
Sterling, Virgina. : Stylus Publishing, 2017. |
Includes bibliographical references and index.
Identifiers: LCCN 2017022658 (print) |
LCCN 2017047549 (ebook) |
ISBN 9781620365267 (uPDF) |
ISBN 9781620365274 (mobi, ePub) |
ISBN 9781620365243 (cloth : alk. paper) |
ISBN 9781620365250 (pbk. : alk. paper) |
ISBN 9781620365267 (library networkable e-edition) |
ISBN 9781620365274 (consumer e-edition)
Subjects: LCSH: Adult education. | Adult education--Cross-cultural studies. | Continuing education. | Continuing education--Cross-cultural studies.
Classification: LCC LC5215 (ebook) | LCC LC5215 .M255 2017 (print) | DDC 374--dc23
LC record available at https://lccn.loc.gov/2017022658

13-digit ISBN: 978-1-62036-524-3 (cloth)
13-digit ISBN: 978-1-62036-525-0 (paperback)
13-digit ISBN: 978-1-62036-526-7 (library networkable e-edition)
13-digit ISBN: 978-1-62036-527-4 (consumer e-edition)

Printed in the United States of America

All first editions printed on acid-free paper
that meets the American National Standards Institute
Z39-48 Standard.

First Edition, 2017

10 9 8 7 6 5 4 3 2 1

CONTENTS

FOREWORD

The rapid-paced changes we are experiencing in our world call for an ongoing conversation to keep adult education relevant, fresh, and current. Two years ago, Stylus Publishing and the American Association for Adult and Continuing Education (AAACE) jointly launched an international compendium to map the field of adult and continuing education. This initiative reflected the commitment of both organizations to assist associations, practitioners, and scholars who contribute to many parts of the adult education field worldwide.

I am pleased to serve as AAACE's president during the timely completion of this important project. I am thankful for the support and contributions of my two predecessors (Margaret Eggleston and Steve Schmidt), as well the publications committee and the board, who initiated and supported the creation of this valuable resource.

The editors successfully attracted an exceedingly diverse group of practitioners and scholars from many countries, types of providers, stages of career, and perspectives. The contributors and editors who helped to create the compendium have given us an extensive resource that will benefit adult educators worldwide. The end product is a useful and accessible tool for adult educators in our continual journey to better our field of study and practice.

The four parts of the compendium are focused on adult learners, teaching and learning, leadership and administration, and inquiry and influences. About 20 brief and substantive articles in each volume refer to related compendium articles and to other publications for more details about the topic. This organization allows each compendium reader to use this map to explore the combination of topics that pertain to their own provider mission and career journey.

I want to offer special thanks to the editors: Alan b. Knox, Simone C. O. Conceição, and Larry G. Martin for their impassioned commitment to this monumental effort. I am confident that your efforts will benefit many in our field and encourage the continual conversation that we call adult education.

On behalf of AAACE, I invite our membership and our many partners worldwide to make use of this excellent resource. Together we will build the future of our field.

Steven B. Frye
President,
American Association for Adult and Continuing Education;
Associate Professor and Interim Director,
School of Interdisciplinary Studies,
Tennessee Technological University

PREFACE

Welcome to this distinctive map of our field. The map was created by and for educators of adults and includes 80 brief and substantive articles. Together, these articles give you access to concepts and examples about various learning opportunities for adults. We hope these examples, concepts, and guidelines will enhance your learning opportunities for adults.

To create this compendium, practitioners and scholars assembled concepts and examples from many countries and types of provider organizations to prepare brief articles that are relevant to your experience and interest in excellent learning opportunities for adults. The table of contents serves as a matrix of potential topics that we used to map the conceptual base of the field. Our matrix was a taxonomy of four parts (learners, teaching, administering, inquiry), each composed of major topic areas and subtopics (concepts) based on the work of numerous practitioners and scholars.

A basic feature of this publication is the ability to follow connections among topics to navigate among articles, discover additional publications, and find ideas to share with program stakeholders. In the electronic edition, hyperlinks allow you to navigate easily among volumes, articles, and keywords so you can create your own individual pathways through the compendium. Connections among articles illustrate important educator decisions related to concepts from several parts of the compendium. For example, helping adults learn is related to participant experience and interests, program coordinator assistance, and available program funding. The compendium includes a glossary to clarify the meanings of terms and concepts for the benefit of readers.

Adult learners vary in what they want to learn and why. The participants in each learning opportunity also vary greatly in experiences, abilities, interests, vocations, ages, responsibilities, and outlooks, all of which influence their lifelong learning activities. Young people may be recipients of education, but as adults, many of them want to be users of education in adult life roles in family, work, and community.

Volumes and Sections

VOLUME ONE: ADULT LEARNERS

Editors: Alan B. Knox, Simone C. O. Conceição, and Larry G. Martin
Sections: Adult Life Cycle Development; Learning Theory and Practice; A Broad Spectrum of Learners

VOLUME TWO: TEACHING AND LEARNING

Editors: Simone C. O. Conceição, Larry G. Martin, and Alan B. Knox
Sections: Multiple Contexts; Approaches to Teaching; Professional Development; Critical Innovation

VOLUME THREE: LEADERSHIP AND ADMINISTRATION

Editors: Larry G. Martin, Simone C. O. Conceição, and Alan B. Knox
Sections: Administration and Coordination; Planning and Resource Allocation; Organizational Change and Culture; Leadership and Vision; Structure and Stakeholders

VOLUME FOUR: INQUIRY AND INFLUENCES

Editors: Alan B. Knox, Simone C. O. Conceição, and Larry G. Martin
Sections: Organizational and Societal Influences; Engaged Inquiry; Methods of Inquiry; Assessment and Evaluation

For each volume, the table of contents and introduction explain to readers the purpose, organization, contents, and contributors. Each article begins with a list of concepts and keywords central to the article. The keywords are all in the index so readers can use the index to locate articles of interest. These features reflect our commitment to a compendium that facilitates individualized inquiry by readers so as to practice what we teach.

Having each of the four volumes of the compendium published separately is a convenience for some readers who may be interested mainly in the contents of that volume.

At the beginning of this preface you were welcomed and introduced to its contents and organization. Similar to a marathon or relay race where the starting line becomes the finish line, we now return full circle, and it is time to pass the baton to you.

Alan B. Knox, Simone C.O. Conceição, and
Larry G. Martin

INTRODUCTION TO VOLUME ONE

Alan B. Knox

The first volume of *Mapping the Field of Adult and Continuing Education: An International Compendium* focuses on adult learners. Contributors from different countries involved with adult education prepared the 16 articles in this volume. These articles can be part of a module or unit in a formal course or serve as resources for practitioners who work with adults. Many of the articles are brief and provide examples and resources for future exploration. Each article contains concepts, examples, implications, keywords, and cross-references to other articles in the compendium. For the e-book version of the compendium, the keywords at the top of the article and cross-references before the references are linked to different parts of the compendium and to the compendium index where interrelated topics can be accessed.

The first section of volume one focuses on adult life cycle development and explains the importance of viewing adult learning from the perspective of the life course of individuals. It also addresses some of the issues and concerns that arise during different phases of life. The five articles in this section include topics on third age, identity/self-development and chronic disease, education of multigenerational groups of adult learners, pseudoautonomy, and learning in later life.

The five articles in the second section of this volume focus on learning theory and practice of adult education. Two articles in this section address transformative learning and neuroscience theories and their implications for the practice of adult education. The other three articles explain relevance of indigenous knowledge, adult literacy practices and adult basic education, and global climate change education.

The six articles in the third section address a broad spectrum of adult learners by focusing on lifelong and lifewide loving in education, adult learners with disabilities, adults with low literacy skills, the power to change lives, gender equity and leadership, and professional development for part-time employees.

The total compendium has four volumes: adult learners (volume one), teaching and learning (volume two), leadership and administration (volume three), and inquiry and influences (volume four). It is published in separate volumes as a convenience for readers who may be interested in the contents of a specific volume. Each volume has its own introduction and a table of contents for the other three volumes is located in the appendix to help the reader identify and read articles of interest located in the other three volumes.

Articles in this volume can help educators of adults and practitioners to discover an effective alignment between learner characteristics and responsive learning activities and enhance their understanding of organized learning opportunities for adults in different contexts. I trust that this volume will encourage educators of adults to explore further learning activities for adult populations with related benefits for their communities.

SECTION ONE

ADULT LIFE CYCLE DEVELOPMENT

Articles in this section focus on various trends and characteristics of adults during the adult life cycle, such as experience, age, generation, health, identity, and self-direction, which shape adult learning and spirit.

I

AN ENGAGED THIRD AGE

Doe Hentschel

Keywords: aging, collaborative, community, engagement, leadership, older adult, projects, third age, training, volunteer

Beatrice was depressed and overwhelmed by family issues she seemed unable to control. In a weak moment, she accepted an invitation to attend a meeting to learn about the Third Age Initiative, a program developed by Leadership Greater Hartford (LGH) for older adults designed to help them find ways to channel their wisdom, knowledge, and experience to strengthen their communities. She acknowledges that she literally dragged herself out of bed because she had made a commitment to attend.

Engagement and Healthy Aging

Beatrice's depression is not unusual in later life. Change and loss that older adults experience as roles evolve, resources become limited, friends and family age and pass away, and they face personal health challenges often lead to withdrawal, lack of self-confidence, and self-deprecation consistent with persistent negative views of aging. At one time, research on adult development indicated that disengagement was the norm for people as they aged.

We now know this need not be the case. Many studies about aging from physical, sociological, and psychological perspectives indicate that active social engagement, intellectual challenges, and purposeful activity contributes to a longer, healthier later life. Healthy aging is characterized by continued growth and development during which aging adults seek learning and experiences that enable them to continue to be engaged in the changing world in ways that affirm their individual relevance and purpose. Rather than a chronological series of events, life more typically evolves in cycles of renewal (Butler, 2005).

Engagement takes many forms. The Corporation for National and Community Service (2007) reports that the benefits to volunteering are measurable and significant. Longevity, increased functioning, and less depression are related to volunteering, especially for older adults. Unfortunately, fewer than one-third of adults over the age of 65 engage in volunteerism, although many who are not engaged indicate they are interested in doing so now or in the future (Zedlewski & Butrica, 2007). Those who are not engaged are sometimes discouraged because volunteer activities available to them are unchallenging or perceived as menial tasks and time fillers. Too often it is because our communities and nonprofit organizations that would benefit from this untapped talent pool do not welcome or understand the resource that older adults represent (Raynor, 2015). Even though many no longer seek or need compensation, frustrated older adults report that they want to continue to "work"—to solve problems, to develop new ideas into projects that have positive results, and to be part of a group that respects each other, collaborates, and learns and grows together. LGH's Third Age Initiative is one of only a handful of programs in the world that attempt to address this need, and it is has been recognized as the premier model for doing so. In 2001, LGH was invited to present a workshop showcasing the program at the United Nations Conference on NGO volunteerism; the following year, the Third Age Initiative was featured at the United Nations' Assembly on Aging in Madrid as a model program to engage older adults as resources in our communities.

The Third Age Initiative

The Third Age Initiative was launched by LGH in 2001 as a vehicle for engaging older adults in their communities. Researching ways in which the quality of life for older adults could be enhanced, a task force in LGH's core program, Quest, concluded that American culture did not value older adults as the treasures that they are. They conceptualized a program to identify, develop, and engage older adults in ways that would tap into their experience and wisdom to strengthen their communities. Unlike more typical programs that train and mobilize older adults as volunteers, this program develops participants' leadership skills. They then take the initiative in addressing community issues through team projects that provide a "learning laboratory" where they exercise the training they have received in collaborative leadership and team building. They focus on issues of interest to them and work together as change agents, program developers, project managers, and policymakers.

Socioeconomic diversity is a unique hallmark of the Third Age Initiative. Zedlewski and Butrica (2007) point out that low income and less educated older adults are less likely to be engaged in the community and therefore less likely to experience the benefits of engagement, such as "decreased mortality and depression, improved health and strength, greater happiness and enhanced cognitive ability" (pp. 2–3). The educational backgrounds of the 341 participants in the 13 classes that have been conducted since 2001 range from less than high school completion to doctoral and professional degrees, with 28% holding less than bachelor's degrees and 22% degrees beyond the master's. Family income is similarly diverse; 23% of all participants report family income of less than $22,500 and 26% report earning more than $75,000. The age range has been 48–88 (21% under the age of 60 and 25% over the age of 70) with 30% men and 70% women. Only 46% are married (others are single, widowed, or divorced), and participants live in Hartford (26%) and 45 other towns in central Connecticut. Approximately 28% represent racial minorities including African American, Hispanic, and West Indian participants. Participants value this diversity and report that the different perspectives, experiences, and skills of their classmates contribute significantly to their positive experience (Broderick, 2016).

Forming the Class

Potential participants respond to broadcast promotional strategies including newspaper articles, television and radio interviews with staff and alumni, the organization's website, and web-based newsletters. Many learn about the program through word-of-mouth and nominations by alumni and other members of the LGH network. Attending an information session precedes submitting an application. The application process is not a vehicle for exclusion; rather, it is a strategy to ensure that marketing activities during the typical six-month recruitment process can be targeted to create a diverse class.

During information sessions, participants are asked what attracted them to this program. The most common motivations include the following: "I have more to give," "I want to find ways to give back," "I want to be involved in the community." One woman who became a member of the first class articulated the following, which others often state as well: "I am busy in retirement; I volunteer, and my husband and I have a full social life. But I am finding that it is difficult to meet new people, and I miss working with others on something that we care about and that we are creating together."

As they learn more about the Third Age Initiative, they recognize how those goals can be achieved.

The Program Design

The Third Age Initiative is a dynamic learning experience highlighted by community action projects. Those projects, carried out by self-directed teams over the course of a year, serve not only to address community needs but also as learning laboratories in collaborative leadership for program participants. A distinguishing characteristic of this program is that it is designed and conducted drawing on a strong foundation of adult education theory and best practices (Eisen, 2005).

The program begins with six weekly, daylong workshops in which class members assess their leadership skills and abilities. Two core components of the curriculum are the Five Practices of Exemplary Leadership® (Kouzes & Posner, 2012) and the Enneagram, a personality system that provides a framework for team building by understanding the perspectives and gifts different personality types can contribute to the work of the team. Training exercises and discussions build on those capacities, particularly in nonhierarchical participative group settings. Interactive activities that are incorporated in each workshop include structured experiences, discussions, and self-assessment instruments. Some workshops include tours in Greater Hartford so that participants learn firsthand about the issues and needs of the community and meet community leaders who are making a difference. At a two-day retreat, they form teams around issues that have been identified by the class using the nominal group process (Hentschel, 1984). They will research these issues and develop and implement projects over the next 10 months while they continue to develop and apply their expertise and perspectives. Bimonthly workshops provide timely learning about group process, inclusive decision making, and leadership for change. Whereas some teams continue their work with their projects after graduation, the program is designed to be a springboard to meaningful community engagement. LGH assists graduates in staying connected to one another, finding community leadership roles, and continuing their leadership development.

Evaluation and Impact

Formative and summative evaluation are conducted in numerous ways. At the conclusion of the retreat, participant satisfaction about the content and process of the six workshops and the two-day retreat is collected. In addition to a 4-point Likert scale on questions related to the content, delivery, and goals of the program (mean scores for the first class ranged from 3.2–3.9 and for the most recent class from 3.7–4.0), participants are asked to rate on a scale of 1 to 10 their learning and their enjoyment of the experience. Scores on these two factors in the first class were 8.81 and 8.83 and have increased incrementally with each class to 9.6 and 9.8 in the most recent class.

Postprogram research demonstrates that, many years later, at least 75% of graduates are involved in the community in ways in which they were not involved before their participation. Engagement ranges from service on non-profit boards, taking on new leadership roles in organizations, running for and getting elected to public office, becoming advocates for various causes, continuing work begun on their teams and even returning to school and beginning new careers. Most graduates attribute their postprogram engagement to their participation in the Third Age Initiative, often through networking as a result of connections made during the program, discovering needs and/or organizations during the class workshops or team process, and developing the skills and/or confidence needed to initiate or respond to opportunities (Eisen, 2012; Leadership Greater Hartford, 2005).

Although team projects are considered the means to the end of later community engagement for program participants, the impact of the three dozen projects completed to date demonstrates how the community benefits from the contributions of these older adults. In 2012, Leadership Greater Hartford recognized projects of Quest task forces and the Third Age Initiative teams that have had the most significant impact on the community. Selected from among hundreds of projects, the Quest taskforce that conceived of the Third Age Initiative and generated the funding to launch it in 2001 received the award for the project that had achieved the greatest overall impact in building community in the 35-year history of LGH. Third Age Initiative team projects received the awards for the greatest impact in Community Development, and Children and Youth. Additionally, finalists in the Basic Needs and Overall Impact categories included Third Age Initiative projects.

Global Implications

Anticipating the impact of tripling the number of people over the age of 60 by the year 2050 to 2 billion, with 400,000 over the age of 80, the United Nations has created an international policy on aging. Central to the 2002 Madrid International Plan of Action on Ageing (2006) is the understanding that "a society for all ages encompasses the goal of providing older persons with the opportunity to continue contributing to society. To work towards this goal, it is necessary to remove whatever excludes or discriminates against them" (p. 639). This document articulates clearly the benefit to individuals and to our societies of healthy aging as described earlier. The plan includes goals to empower older people so that they can be productively engaged through work and volunteerism and to provide opportunities for them to continue to develop, learn, contribute to their communities, and fulfill their potential. In 2010, the United Nations created the Open-Ended Working Group on Aging, which meets annually to work on the implementation of the 2002 Madrid Plan. Review of the most recent papers from the working group indicates that their current focus is on the need for human rights to extend to older people, especially those in developing countries and particularly women who are disproportionately discriminated against.

Replication

Six years after dragging herself out of bed, Beatrice, now 69, works part-time as a patient advocate with an organization that addresses the needs of citizens who suffer from sickle cell anemia. She reengaged with a prestigious local organization that provides training in the arts and culture of the African Diaspora, and last year served as chair of its board of directors. She continues the work that her Third Age Initiative team began to support the reentry of formerly incarcerated individuals into the community, and she regularly attends LGH's events and workshops. Beatrice sees her participation in the Third Age Initiative as a launching pad that helped her find a way to give back to the community.

As effective as the Third Age Initiative is as a strategy that successfully achieves the goals established by the United Nations, sustainability and replication are challenging. Several other community leadership organizations in the United States have implemented similar programs to engage older adults in community leadership. Unlike the Third Age Initiative, these programs focus on professional retirees and graduates of their leadership programs for midcareer professionals. The socioeconomic diversity that characterizes the LGH program, which is completely funded by grants and donations and charges no tuition, has not been replicated in these programs, nor is there a similar emphasis on developing new leadership skills.

Zedlewski and Butrica (2007) call for policy interventions and more funding for training programs that will help connect older adults to meaningful engagement. Historic ageism is a well-recognized barrier. A new initiative involving the American Association for Retired Persons, the American Federation for Aging Research, the American Geriatrics Society, the American Society on Aging, the Gerontological Society of America, Grantmakers in Aging, the National Council on Aging, and the National Hispanic Council on Aging working with the Frameworks Institute is aimed at greater understanding of today's older adults.

The United Nations challenges us to embrace aging "as an achievement" rather than a burden and calls for humane societies to recognize that the experiences and resources of the higher age groups are a benefit to us all. The Third Age Initiative can serve as a prototype for those societies seeking to draw on the assets of older citizens.

Suggested Cross-References

For more information on concepts and ideas discussed in this article, please see the following articles in the compendium: 5, 6, 10, 11, 19, 35, 52, 57, 66, 67, 70, 78, 80

References

Broderick, M. (October 2016). "Older adults giving back: Leadership Greater Hartford's program drives volunteerism." *Hartford Magazine.* Retrieved from http://www.courant.com/hartford-magazine/features/hc-hm-nh-transitions-third-age-initiative-20160928-story.html

Butler, C. B. (2005). Age-related paradigms. *New Directions for Adult and Continuing Education, 2005*(108), 61–68.

Corporation for National and Community Service, Office of Research and Policy Development. (2007). *The health benefits of volunteering: A review of recent research.* Washington DC.

Eisen, M. J. (2005, Winter). Shifts in the landscape of learning: New challenges, new opportunities. In M. A. Wolf, "Adulthood new terrain," *New Directions for Adult and Continuing Education, 108*, 15–26.

Eisen, M. J. (2012). *The third age initiative: The first ten years.* Unpublished report, Leadership Greater Hartford, Hartford, CT.

Hentschel, D. (1984). There's a method in the magic: The nominal group process. *Lifelong Learning: An Omnibus of Practice and Research, 8*(4), 11–26.

Kouzes, J. M., & Posner, B. Z. (2012). *The leadership challenge* (5th ed.). San Francisco, CA: John Wiley and Sons.

Leadership Greater Hartford. (2005). *Community involvement analysis.* Unpublished report, Hartford, CT.

Madrid Political Declaration and International Plan of Action on Ageing, 2002. (2006). *International Social Science Journal, 58*(190), 633–665.

Raynor, B. (2015). "Ageism in action? Ageism inaction!" *Generations*, retrieved from http://asaging.org/blog/ageism-action-ageism-inaction

Zedlewski, S. R., & Butrica, B. A. (2007, December). Are we taking full advantage of older adults' potential? *Perspectives on Productive Aging, 9,* 1–7.

2

IDENTITY/ SELF-DEVELOPMENT AND CHRONIC DISEASE

Lisa M. Baumgartner

Keywords: chronic disease, chronic illness, identity, self

The purpose of this article is to show the interrelationship between chronic diseases and identity development. Statistics on chronic disease will be followed by an examination of the philosophical underpinnings of identity models. Chronic disease identity models and common themes in the chronic illness literature will be reviewed. Last, I will consider possibilities for future research.

Chronic diseases last three months or more and cannot be prevented or cured (National Health Council, 2016). In 2012, 38 million of the 56 million deaths that occurred worldwide were due to chronic illnesses (Global Health Observatory, n.d.). Half of all adults in the United States have at least one chronic health condition and 25% have two or more chronic diseases (Ward, Schiller, & Goodman, 2012). Chronic diseases include such illnesses as diabetes, asthma, cancer, heart disease, arthritis, and obesity ("Living with a chronic illness," 2016).

Given that chronic disease is part of the context of many people's lives, and identity development is lifelong, it makes sense that knowing more about how chronic disease influences identity development would help individuals understand more about themselves and how they can live with chronic disease.

Philosophical Underpinnings of Identity Models

Before examining the philosophical underpinnings of identity models, some definitions of terms are necessary. Whereas some scholars use *self* and *identity* interchangeably, others believe that *self* concerns one's interior world and *identity* describes "the properties of sameness and distinction that link the interior world of psychological experience and the exterior world of language and categorization" (Hammack, 2015, p. 12). The chronic illness literature has both made distinctions between these words and used them interchangeably.

The definitions of *identity* belie their historical and philosophical roots. Philosophical perspectives on identity focused on the importance of "*memory, meaning, relationality* and the perception of *sameness or difference*" (Hammack, 2015, p. 13, emphasis in original). These concepts are fundamental to the foundational theorists of identity research, William James and George Herbert Mead. American psychologist William James focused on the sameness and continuity of the self and the integration of mind, emotion, and the body as part of one's identity where the private interior self interacts with society. Theories that originate this theoretical base include Erik Erikson's eight-stage model of psychosocial development; James Marcia's identity status model; Cross's stage-based, Black identity development model; Helms's White identity model; and narrative identity development (Hammack, 2015). For example, Erik Erikson (1980) said that identity was "a persistent sameness within oneself (self-sameness) and a persistent sharing of some kind of essential character with others" (p. 109). The social environment influences our identity. Erik Erikson (1968) stated that identity is located "*in the core of the communal individual* and yet also *in the core of the communal culture*" (p. 22, emphasis in original).

Another theoretical concept of identity comes from Herbert Mead who focused on how the social context and interactions with others influenced identity and how different identities (e.g., identity/role as mother, sister, worker) interacted in the social context (Hammack, 2015). Identity theorists whose ideas are derived from this perspective include Goffman's stigma and identity management and Stryker and Burke's identity theory where individuals possess multiple roles (e.g., drummer, teacher, friend) whose salience is determined by the social context (Hammack, 2015). Roles enacted across various contexts are more salient than roles that are enacted in fewer contexts (Stryker & Burke, 2000). For example, a person may claim the role of being a professor across many contexts, but her role as a bass guitar player in a garage band may be less salient.

Models of Chronic Illness Identity/Self-Development

Several models of chronic illness pertain to identity/self-development. Kelly and Field's (1996) crisis model is concerned with changes in identity.

Identity is considered the known or "public and shared aspects of individuals. Identity establishes what and where the person is within social structures" (p. 245). If one's chronic illness becomes visible then issues of stigma, labelling, a status passage from a person considered "healthy" to "unhealthy," and a change of status in the social structure are concerns (Kralik, Koch, & Eastwood, 2003). Scholars have discussed status passages in people living with HIV (PLWHAs; Sandstrom, 1990) and rheumatoid arthritis (Kristiansen & Antoft, 2016). Kelly and Field's (1996) negotiation model of chronic illness focuses on the loss of the normal self and wanting to maintain a normal self in the face of a changing body. The self is the "existential me" (Kralik et al., 2003, p. 14). The self must negotiate with the illness identity, and there is a struggle to remain normal. Chronic illness is considered a "biographical disruption" (Bury, 1982, p. 167), and individuals want to return to a normal state. This framework has been used in qualitative studies such as chronic obstructive pulmonary disease (COPD; Jowsey, Yen, Bagheri, & McRae, 2014).

Although not explicitly related to identity development, Frank's (1995) three types of illness narratives can be uncovered in the identity development journeys of the chronically ill. The restitution narrative states, "yesterday I was healthy, today I'm sick, but tomorrow I'll be healthy again" (p. 77). The chaos narrative imagines "life is never getting better" (p. 97). The individual feels a complete lack of control personally, and there may be a sense that no one (including doctors) knows what is going on. Last, individuals who tell quest narratives "meet suffering head on; they accept illness and seek to *use* it" (p. 115). Quest narratives can be related as a memoir where the illness is interspersed with details from one's life. Alternately, those who relate their quest narrative as a manifesto turn a critical eye on society and illness and call for social justice. In the automythology quest narrative, there is a personal reinvention due to the illness. Individuals emerge with a new identity in some cases (Frank, 1995). Frank's model has been used as the theoretical framework in several studies including research concerning chronic fatigue syndrome (Whitehead, 2006).

Common Themes in the Chronic Illness and Identity Literature

There are several themes that are commonly found in the chronic illness and identity literature. Transitions and the role of support in the chronic illness identity process are discussed. These themes are explained in the following sections.

Transitions

Transitions affect identity. A meta-analysis of the health literature revealed that the term *transition* was used to describe a transition from health to illness or a change within an illness, such as having to start treatment (Kralik, Visentin, & Van Loon, 2006). The literature defined *transition* most often as a "passage between two points" or the need to adapt to or integrate an illness. Additionally, transition "involves a process of inner-reorientation" (p. 324) as a person adapts to a new situation, such as a chronic illness. Transition also informed changes in self and identity. For example, a stroke may cause a woman to reconsider her identity (Hilton, 1998). Kralik and colleagues (2006) noted that transition is both a linear and a recurring process with losses and gains that require readjustment.

Paterson's (2001) shifting perspectives model of chronic illness resulted from a metasynthesis of 292 qualitative research reports concerning "chronic physical illness" (p. 21). This model delineates the following perspectives: (a) illness in the foreground, (b) wellness in the foreground, (c) shifting from wellness to illness in the foreground, and (d) shifting from illness to wellness in the foreground. When the *illness is in the foreground*, it is all-consuming. Typically, dealing with symptoms and learning about the disease are common during this time. When individuals experience *wellness in the foreground*, one's identity is not the diseased body but other facets such as one's spirituality or social commitments. Individuals shift from *wellness to illness* when they detect a lack of control of the disease such as "disease progression, lack of skill to manage the disease, disease-related stigma and interactions with others that emphasize dependence and hopelessness" (p. 24). When there is a shift from *illness to wellness* in the foreground, there is generally renewed hope, yet the illness still requires monitoring.

Kralik (2002) described a transition process of midlife women living with a chronic illness. She interviewed 81 women over the course of a year. Kralik found that when first confronted with the illness women experienced "an extraordinary phase of turmoil and distress" (p. 149). They transitioned to ordinariness or incorporation of their illness into their lives and identities with the help of others who encouraged them. With this encouragement and empowerment, they found a place for the illness in their lives. They recognized they needed to think differently about the disease and adjust their expectations.

The Importance of Support in the Identity Incorporation Process

Another theme in the chronic illness and identity literature is that this process does not occur in a vacuum. Support from others in the form of conversations with family, friends, and/or support groups is integral to incorporating a chronic illness into one's identity. This support is often necessary at diagnosis and during transitions as individuals grapple with changing physical abilities and, in some cases, as with individuals living with HIV/AIDS, the stigma of the disease (Hayes, Vaughan, Medeiros, & Dubuque, 2002). Disclosure is integral to the integration of chronic illness into one's identity and finding the right person or support group is imperative in the identity integration process (Baumgartner & David, 2009).

Conclusions and Future Research

Although the identity and chronic illness literature has informed theory and practice, there are several ways this research can generally be improved. First, the use of explicit theoretical frameworks is imperative for further development of identity theories related to chronic illness. Second, a clear definition of *identity* is needed in some studies as the concepts of self and identity are often interchanged. Third, much of the identity and chronic illness literature does not explicitly discuss the impact of positionalities such as race; class; gender; culture; and such things as historical, chronological, or developmental time on how chronic illness affects the self and identity. Last, most of the studies on chronic illness and identity are cross-sectional. More longitudinal studies on the effect of chronic illnesses on identity over time are needed.

Chronic diseases affect millions of individuals. New therapies and medications mean people are living longer with perhaps more than one chronic illness. To help individuals live their best lives, attention to how these illnesses affect individuals' identities and selves is imperative. Although research has been done in this area, future research is needed to strengthen the applicability of current models and to provide health educators and practitioners practical ways to assist their clients in navigating their identity with a chronic disease.

Suggested Cross-References

For more information on concepts and ideas discussed in this article, please see the following articles in the compendium: 5, 6, 11, 12, 28, 34, 35, 52, 76, 77, 80

References

Baumgartner, L. M., & David, K. N. (2009). Accepting being poz: The incorporation of the HIV identity into the self. *Qualitative Health Research, 19*(12), 1730–1743.

Bury, M. (1982). Chronic illness as a biographical disruption. *Sociology of Health and Illness, 4,* 165–182.

Erikson, E. H. (1968). *Identity, youth, and crisis.* New York, NY: W. W. Norton Company.

Erikson, E. H. (1980). *Identity and the life cycle.* New York, NY: W. W. Norton Company.

Frank, A. W. (1995). *The wounded storyteller: Body, illness, and ethics.* Chicago, IL: The University of Chicago Press.

Global Health Observatory. (n.d.). *Noncommunicable diseases (NCD).* World Health Organization. Retrieved from http://www.who.int/gho/ncd/en/

Hammack, P. L. (2015). Theoretical foundations of identity. In K. C. McLean & M. Syed (Eds.), *The Oxford handbook of identity development* (pp. 11–30). Oxford, England: Oxford University Press.

Hayes, R. A., Vaughan, C., Medeiros, T., & Dubuque, E. (2002). Stigma directed toward chronic illness is resistant to change through education and exposure. *Psychological Reports, 90,* 1161–1173.

Hilton, E. (1998). The meaning of stroke in elderly women: A phenomenological investigation. *Journal of Gerontological Nursing, 28*(7), 19–26.

Jowsey, T., Yen., L. E., Bagheri, N., & McRae, I. (2014). Time spent by people managing chronic obstructive pulmonary disease indicates biographical disruption. *International Journal of Chronic Obstructive Pulmonary Disease, 9,* 87–97.

Kelly, M. P., & Field, D. (1996). Medical sociology, chronic illness, and the body. *Sociology of Health and Illness, 18*(2), 241–257.

Kralik, D. (2002). The quest for ordinariness: Transition experienced by midlife women living with chronic illness. *Journal of Advanced Nursing, 39*(2), 146–154.

Kralik, D., Koch, T., & Eastwood, S. (2003). The salience of the body: Transition in sexual self-identity for women living with multiple sclerosis. *Journal of Advanced Nursing, 42*(1), 11–20.

Kralik, D., Visentin, K., & van Loon, A. (2006). Transition: A literature review. *Journal of Advanced Nursing, 55*(3), 320–329.

Kristiansen, T. M., & Antoft, R. (2016). Patient education as a status passage in life: An ethnographic study exploring participation in a Danish group based patient education programme. *Social Science & Medicine, 158,* 34–42.

"Living with a chronic illness." (2016). Medline Plus, U.S. National Library of Medicine. Retrieved from https://medlineplus.gov/ency/patientinstructions/000602.htm

National Health Council. (2016). About chronic conditions. Retrieved from http://www.nationalhealthcouncil.org/newsroom/about-chronic-conditions

Paterson, B. L. (2001). The shifting perspectives model of chronic illness. *Journal of Nursing Scholarship, 33*(1), 21–26.

Sandstrom, K. L. (1990). Confronting deadly disease: The drama of identity construction among gay men with AIDS. *Journal of Contemporary Ethnography, 19,* 271–294.

Stryker, S., & Burke, P. J. (2000). The past, present and future of an identity theory. *Social Psychology Quarterly, 63*(4), 284–297. Retrieved from http://www.jstor.org/stable/2695840

Ward, B. W., Schiller, J. S., & Goodman, R. A. (2012). Multiple chronic conditions among US adults. *Preventing Chronic Disease: Public Health Research, Practice, and Policy, 11*, 1–4. doi:10.5888/pcd11.130389

Whitehead, L. C. (2006). Quest, chaos, and restitution: Living with chronic fatigue syndrome/myalgic encephalomyelitis. *Social Science and Medicine, 62,* 2236–2245.

3

EDUCATING MULTIGENERATIONAL GROUPS OF ADULT LEARNERS

Andrea Nikischer

Keywords: diversity, disabilities, learning preferences, Millennials, multigenerational, wellness, workforce

In the United States and across the globe adult education learning spaces include students spanning multiple generations. Members of these generations bring a wealth of unique life experiences and perspectives with them when they work and learn. Generational differences have the power to impact student learning preferences, with important implications for educators and employers.

Generational Groups

Generational groups are created when people are born during a similar time period and experience major economic, political, technological, and/or world events together. Four major generational groups[1] currently participate in adult and workplace education in the United States, as discussed in the following sections (see Boysen, Daste, & Northern, 2016; Fry, 2015; Helyer & Lee, 2012; Hershatter & Epstein, 2010).

Traditionalists: Born 1928–1945

Members of the oldest and most experienced group, the Traditionalists or Silents, tend to share a traditional view of education and work. As most Traditionalists are no longer in the workplace, they seek adult education opportunities primarily for personal fulfillment.

Baby Boomers: Born 1946–1964

Baby Boomers were born after World War II and are seen as loyal and hard-working. They seek learning opportunities in order to stay competitive in an uncertain economic climate and to overcome any perceived limitations associated with age. As with Traditionalists, Boomers did not grow up with technology and are, in general, less naturally adept at its use.

Generation X: Born 1965–1980

Gen Xers are in the early to middle stages of their careers and many find themselves faced with challenges associated with caring both for younger children and aging parents. Xers are often described as independent and committed to challenging the status quo.

Millennials: Born 1981–1997

Members of the youngest group, Millennials[2] are the most technologically savvy generation. Considered "digital natives" (Prensky, 2001), this generation was the first to live their entire life connected to digital devices and the Internet. Due to this experience, Millennials learn new technology easily and often show a strength and preference for multitasking. They appreciate clearly outlined objectives and request consistent and timely feedback.

The Current Educational Landscape

The U.S. Department of Education's National Center for Education Statistics (2016) projects that the number of students aged 25 and older who are enrolled in higher education will increase faster than traditional college-aged students during 2014 to 2024. Workplace education will also have to accommodate generational diversity. According to the Pew Research Center, more than one-third of workers in the United States are Millennials. These young employees join Generation X (34%), Baby Boomers (29%), and a small number of Traditionalists (2%) to create the most generationally diverse workforce in history (Fry, 2015). Global workforce trends indicate a similar pattern of age and generation diversification, as older workers remain in the global workforce up to and past retirement age and fewer younger workers enter[3] (Society for Human Resource Management Foundation, 2015).

Beyond formal education, 73% of adults in the United States label themselves as lifelong learners, engaging in a variety of nonformal and informal forms of adult education. Whereas younger adults participate at the highest levels, a full 62% of adults aged 65 and older continue to participate in adult learning opportunities (Horrigan, 2016).

Best Practices for Working With Multigenerational Groups

Extensive scholarship has been produced related to working with multigenerational (also known as cross-generational) groups of adults. A key facet of this work is the focus on creating learning spaces and workplaces that respect and value generational differences and allow each group to maximize its strengths (Sánchez & Kaplan, 2014).

Consistent recommendations across literature include (a) finding ways to leverage the life experience of older learners and the technological skills of younger learners to create robust cross-generational learning communities, (b) providing two-way mentorship opportunities between older learners and Millennials, and (c) diversifying instruction to meet the needs of each individual learner (Boysen et al., 2016; Cekada, 2012; Helyer & Lee, 2012; Hershatter & Epstein, 2010; Torrico Meruvia, 2013).

Future Directions

Research in the area of multigenerational learning should continue. As the "post-Millennial" (Fry, 2015) generation begins to enter adult education learning spaces, stakeholders will need to learn about members of this group. Additionally, although researchers often focus efforts on the youngest group of adult learners, older adults should not be ignored. Morris (2014) argues that more attention needs to be paid to the oldest members of our learning communities. Research in this area should explore older students' needs related both to generation and age.

Final Thoughts

Increases in diversity based on ethnicity, gender identification, socioeconomic status, age, and generation provide a strong foundation for rich adult learning experiences. Stakeholders need to recognize the variety of perspectives adults bring with them to their learning in order to create positive learning opportunities.

Suggested Cross-References

For more information on concepts and ideas discussed in this article, please see the following articles in the compendium: 5, 7, 15, 19, 33, 49, 57, 71

Notes

1. In addition to the groups listed is a group known as *cuspers*. Cuspers were born at the end or beginning of one generation but share the experiences of another, thus, they do not fit neatly into a generational category (Johnson & Lopes, 2008). It is important to note that generational grouping is not a strict science and individual life experiences may play a greater role than experiences associated with a generational category.

2. A separate, smaller generation known as Generation Y is considered part of the larger Millennial generational group. Generation Y is the oldest of the Millennials and shares some characteristics with Generation X.

3. Notable variations exist across continents and countries, including in Africa, where the percentage of young workers entering the workforce remains high.

References

Boysen, P. G., Daste, L., & Northern, T. (2016). Multigenerational challenges and the future of graduate medical education. *The Ochsner Journal, 16*(1), 101.

Cekada, T. L. (2012). Training a multigenerational workforce. *Professional Safety, 57*(3), 40.

Fry, R. (2015). Millennials surpass Gen Xers as the largest generation in U.S. labor force. Pew Research Center. Retrieved from http://www.pewresearch.org/fact-tank/2015/05/11/millennials-surpass-gen-xers-as-the-largest-generation-in-u-s-labor-force/ft_15-05-04_genlaborforcecomposition-2/

Helyer, R., & Lee, D. (2012). The twenty first century multiple generation workforce. *Education + Training, 54*(7), 565–578.

Hershatter, A., & Epstein, M. (2010). Millennials and the world of work: An organization and management perspective. *Journal of Business and Psychology, 25*(2), 211–223.

Horrigan, J. B. (2016). Lifelong learning and technology. Pew Research Center. Retrieved from http://www.pewinternet.org/2016/03/22/the-joy-and-urgency-of-learning/

Johnson, J. A., & Lopes, J. (2008). The intergenerational workforce, revisited. *Organization Development Journal, 26*(1), 31–36.

Morris, L. V. (2014). The mixed generation classroom: What does the research tell us? *Innovative Higher Education*, 39(4), 261–262. doi:10.1007/s10755-014-9301-8

Prensky, M. (2001). Digital natives, digital immigrants part 1. *On the Horizon, 9*(5), 1–6.

Sánchez, M., & Kaplan, M. (2014). Intergenerational learning in higher education: Making the case for multigenerational classrooms. *Educational Gerontology, 40*(7), 473–485.

Society for Human Resource Management Foundation. (2015). *Global trends impacting the future of HR management: Engaging and integrating a global workforce*. The Economist Intelligence Unit Limited. Retrieved from http://futurehrtrends.eiu.com/report-2015/profile-of-the-global-workforce-present-and-future/

Torrico Meruvia, R. T. (2013, Winter). Navigating a multigenerational workforce in child welfare. *Practice Perspective*, 1–6. Retrieved from https://www.socialworkers.org/assets/secured/documents/practice/children/Child%20Welfare%20Multigenerational%20Workforce.pdf

U.S. Department of Education, National Center for Education Statistics. (2016). *Digest of education statistics, 2014* (NCES 2016-006), Chapter 3. Retrieved from http://nces.ed.gov/pubs2016/2016006_3.pdf

4

PSEUDOAUTONOMY IN THE LIVES OF ADULT LEARNERS

Robert Jecklin

Keywords: learner autonomy, learner control, personal autonomy, self-determination, self-direction, self-motivation, societal transformation

Educators and researchers may find it helpful to consider the role of pseudoautonomy in the lives of adults as they learn in formal, non-formal, and informal settings. Twenty-five years ago, in the book *Self-Direction for Lifelong Learning*, Australian Philip C. Candy (1991) concluded that thinking and acting autonomously were important characteristics of adult life, and that adult educators considered the facilitation of learner autonomy to be an important part of their work. Candy conceptualized learner autonomy as a readiness to self-direct thought, action, and learning in specific situations.

Recognizing Pseudoautonomy and Related Consequences

According to Candy (1991), learners experienced *pseudoautonomy* in situations where educators communicated learner-controlled pedagogy while exemplifying, in their actions, an instructor-controlled pedagogy. Candy conceded that "it is difficult for an instructor to feel committed to a situation in which the prerogatives for objective-setting; selecting content, pacing, and sequence; and carrying out evaluation have all been ceded to learners" (p. 237). Candy believed that learners lived with pseudoautonomy in learning situations because instructors lacked the skills or commitment to support learner control of instruction. Another influence might be that external pressures on the instructor to demonstrate a controlling pedagogy could have led them to feel accountable for the intent, content, pacing, sequence, and outcome of the learning. Candy also recognized that more authentic learner control could disturb the personal equilibrium of the learner, an equilibrium based on beliefs and practices acquired through years of instruction where learners usually responded to the demands of instructor-controlled learning.

Candy (1991) conceded that instruction based on pseudoautonomy did not necessarily interfere with adult acquisition of information; instead, he warned that adults who experienced pseudoautonomy were at risk for diminished curiosity, less critical thought, less retention of what was important to learners, and other qualitative differences in adult learning. Candy suggested that researchers and other educators would better understand how to develop and support learner control of instruction and related learning outcomes if they used a constructivist framework to understand instructional situations from the perspectives of both instructors and learners.

Learner Experience With Pseudoautonomy

Because pseudoautonomy is a compromise between instructor ideology and instructor practice, learners may not notice a lack of support for their control of a learning situation and conflicted educators seem unlikely to bring this deficit to the learner's attention. Other learners may experience unsettling dissonance as conflicted instructors seek to control objectives, content, pacing, sequence, and/or the ongoing evaluation of their learning. Some learners seek personal equilibrium by challenging instructor control, whereas other learners surrender to instructor control. In addition to the direct influence of the instructor skills, learners experience pseudoautonomy through the less direct influence of external forces found in specific learning situations.

Consider the forces involved in welfare reform as a cause of pseudoautonomy in the lives of some adult learners. Sparks (2001) described how adult basic education (ABE) was an important but unappreciated part of welfare reform. She wrote that "ABE practitioners now find themselves left out of the loop of decision making, both at the policy level and the recipient level" (p. 148). Sparks also highlighted how learners experienced resentment after being denied control over decisions about the purpose, content, sequence, pacing, or value of their learning situations.

Consider how workers may experience pseudoautonomy as employers define workplace learning situations. Peterson (2010) presents an enlightened perspective on contemporary workplace learning emphasizing participatory approaches such as apprenticeships, on-the-job training, quality circles, and career and leadership development; although workers may find these beneficial it is also likely that learner control is limited when learning does not reflect the interests of the sponsoring employer. Peterson also admits how discrimination and exclusion can undermine learner control in workplace learning. Spencer (2010) provides a more critical perspective on worker control of workplace learning. More blunt than Peterson, Spencer writes that "many situations describing workers undertaking their own learning are more accurately described as responses to manager and supervisor prompting" (p. 257), and that worker control of union-organized learning in the workplace is diluted by a global context where management can move beyond union influence.

Consider low-income citizens involved in education for financial literacy who may be experiencing pseudoautonomy as they are encouraged to save money they do not have, plan for losing a job they do not have, consider retirement before they have had a productive work life, and plan for disasters without the necessary resources. English (2014) describes how both the governments of Canada and the United States have funded and otherwise encouraged programs to educate their poorest citizens about how to live a middle-class life. She writes about the socioeconomic and cultural forces that encourage this mismatch between what the participants might choose to learn and what has been chosen for them. She advocates for more learner control, stating:

> What does it mean to be involved in a literacy initiative that never seeks the views of the community it serves in terms of readiness to learn, appropriateness of material, etc.? And, we need to question our assumption that all literacy efforts are being used for benign purposes. (p. 54)

Pseudoautonomy Beyond the Isolated Instructor–Learner Relationship

Researchers and practitioners might find it helpful to think about pseudoautonomy beyond the power sharing between teacher and learner. Brookfield (2005) uses ideology critique to foster the "ideal of learners making autonomous choices among multiple possibilities" and he emphasizes "that we cannot stand outside the social, cultural, and political streams within which we swim" (pp. 83–84). In a sense, Candy might be agreeing with Brookfield's broader perspective when he offered that self-direction was not only for self-fulfillment but also for societal transformation.

In Brookfield's (2010) writing about democratic leadership, the democratic process requires education and learning where the roles of teacher and learner rapidly shift from one participant to another, "trusting the extraordinary knowledge of ordinary people and working to ensure that those affected by decisions have the most powerful voices in those decisions and have access to all relevant knowledge" (p. 5). In this broader, more collective learning situation, it is still possible to experience pseudoautonomy because of the influence of external forces on any individual or group of participants, and it is still important to assure facilitation by and for ordinary people.

Suggested Cross-References

For more information on concepts and ideas discussed in this article, please see the following articles in the compendium: 2, 8, 11, 72, 76, 79

References

Brookfield, S. (2005). *The power of critical theory: Liberating adult learning and teaching*. San Francisco, CA: Jossey-Bass.

Brookfield, S. (2010). Leading democratically. *New Directions for Adult & Continuing Education, 2010* (128), 5–13.

Candy, P. C. (1991). *Self-direction for lifelong learning*. San Francisco, CA: Jossey-Bass.

English, L. M. (2014). Financial literacy: A critical adult education appraisal. *New Directions for Adult & Continuing Education, 2014*(141), 47–55.

Peterson, S. (2010). Employer-sponsored learning in the workplace. In C. E. Kasworm, A. D. Rose, & J. M. Ross-Gordon (Eds.), *Handbook of adult and continuing education* (2010 ed.; pp. 243–252). Thousand Oaks, CA: American Association for Adult and Continuing Education and SAGE.

Sparks, B. (2001). Adult basic education, social policy, and educator's concerns: The influence of welfare reform on practice. *Adult Basic Education, 11*(3), 135.

Spencer, B. (2010). Worker's education for the 21st century. In C. E. Kasworm, A. D. Rose, & J. M. Ross-Gordon (Eds.), *Handbook of adult and continuing education* (2010 ed.; pp. 253–262). Thousand Oaks, CA: American Association for Adult and Continuing Education and SAGE.

5

LEARNING IN LATER LIFE

Brian Findsen

Keywords: critical gerontology, educational gerontology, later life learning, older adults, seniors' education, third age

The phrase "learning in later life" has assumed major significance for educators and allied professionals in their efforts to understand the dynamics of learning for older people across the globe. In earlier times, the phrase "educational gerontology" was used to describe a similar set of ideas but is now deemed too restrictive for the vast range of learning in which seniors participate, whether organized *for* them or *with* them, or self-initiated. The purpose of this article is to provide a solid platform for conceptualizing the complex array of learning opportunities open to older adults in diverse cultural contexts.

Fundamentally, later life can be interpreted in different ways across and within cultures. There is no benchmark chronological age at which a person may become an older adult (Phillipson, 2013), though many nations signal this transition through the award of pensions in accord with a social welfare regime. For instance, in Aotearoa, New Zealand, there is a universal pension available to all citizens at age 65 regardless of gender, ethnicity, or other social attributes, but this is not the case in many countries and societies. Hence, older adulthood is context-specific (Phillipson, 1998). Within the scope of later life, there are vast developmental and social distinctions between young-old and old-old (Neugarten, 1976); people entering retirement at age 60, for instance, are likely to have very different (learning) needs from individuals in their 90s. Hence, heterogeneity among older people should be acknowledged. Laslett (1991), in describing the *third age*—typically one of increased freedom to spend time less encumbered with the multiple responsibilities of the *second age* (entering and/or sustaining a career; building a family; striving for financial security)—has identified the considerable period of life beyond paid work in which adults continue to learn. The *fourth age*, often neglected by the majority of society (Formosa & Higgs, 2013), is one of returning to dependence and preparation for death.

A significant distinction needs to be made between *learning* and *education*. On the one hand, learning can occur anywhere and anytime for an individual, aligned to one's chosen pattern of living. It is both lifelong and lifewide (Findsen & Formosa, 2011), synonymous with life itself. We learn as we live. On the other hand, *education* refers to learning that is systematically organized, often credentialed and hierarchically constructed and frequently associated with an agency/provider. This distinction for (older) adults is important because learning is often self-directed and individualistic and not necessarily aligned to an organization's objectives. Further, we need to distinguish among informal learning (often incidental and unintentional), nonformal education (that which is organized, frequently in an organizational context—for instance, associated with volunteering for a social agency)—and formal education (usually assessed and for credit, led by a teacher in an education setting). For the majority of seniors, learning is informal or nonformal, away from universities and vocational institutes (Withnall, 2010).

Motivation and Needs Assessment

The motivations for learning for older people have been fairly comprehensively examined. Drawing on the well-known typology of learning needs devised by Howard McClusky (1974), these needs reflect different aspects of older people's lives. He distinguished needs as follows:

- *Coping* needs: adults engaged in economic sufficiency, physical fitness, and basic education
- *Expressive* needs: adults learning for their own sake, where creativity is emphasised
- *Contributive* needs: adults engaging actively in society as contributors (not just as consumers)
- *Influence* needs: adults becoming politicized to effect social change
- *Transcendence* needs: adults achieving an advanced state of consciousness

Although it is common for people in later life to spend larger periods of time on coping and expressive needs fulfilment, the two other domains should not be minimized in importance. Increasingly, older people want to "pay back" to society, commonly in volunteering roles (Newman & Hatton-Yeo, 2008), their labor often propping up fledgling not-for-profit, socially oriented agencies. Further, as the numbers of people over the age of 60 increase in most nations (Tuckett & McAulay, 2005), their physical presence cannot be ignored, and, indeed, their political force is something that governments ignore at their peril (see the actions of Grey Power, an explicitly political organization that advocates for the rights of older people). Another way in which older persons' needs have been described is in the continuum from expressive to instrumental (Jarvis, 2001). From a humanistic perspective (e.g., Laslett's third-age description), the focus of later life is on leisure-oriented endeavors. Arguably, this is a highly romanticized view of later life. The neoliberal economic-political context in which many older people conduct their lives is one of enduring hardship as governments find it difficult to sustain a social benefit for elders. Instead, the reality for many older people—often regarded as a marginalized group in society (Findsen, 2005)—is that they need to continue in the workforce for as long as feasible to maximize their economic futures. Those from working-class backgrounds may find themselves locked out of job opportunities where, for example, information and communication technology (ICT) competencies are high in demand.

Provision of Learning Opportunities

The issue of participation in education for older adults is long-standing. The truism that "those who have, get more" applies strongly in older adult education. People in earlier life who have established considerable human and social capital (Field, 2003) are usually adept at arranging their own education later in life because they have the requisite skills and social networks to acquire further nonformal or formal education. It is important to note that older adults have access to educational programs designed for the general public, although these may have been designed without seniors being a target for the program. Hence, it is possible to envisage education agencies according to the extent to which older people feature as incidental and/or primary targets of the program. At one extreme, an agency may focus almost exclusively on older people (for example, Seniornet), and on another, seniors might be invisible in planning or engagement (Findsen, 2005). However, there is a strand of provision that is self-initiated, typified by the establishment of the University of the Third Age (U3A), where the learning is controlled by older people themselves; the program itself relates to their own learning needs, the program is taught by members themselves, the administration is minimal, and the costs are intentionally kept low. In effect, it epitomizes peer learning of seniors for seniors. On the other hand, the U3A has been heavily critiqued for its cultural insensitivity, middle-class bias, and conservatism (Formosa, 2000).

Recent and Future Developments

Learning in later life has developed a much more critical edge in the most recent decade, linked to *critical educational gerontology* (Battersby, 1987; Glendenning, 2000). In addition, its internationalization has been quite rapid (e.g., see Boulton-Lewis & Tam, 2012; Findsen & Formosa, 2016). Emergent issues in this field have focused on the strengthening links between health and learning, obviously because in later life health is a dominant personal and societal matter (Aldridge & Lavender, 2000). In the context of family learning, intergenerational learning/education has assumed more significance (see Schmidt-Hertha, Krasovec, & Formosa, 2014). As more people in most nations have increased life expectancy, the issue of third-age learning gains more prominence (Formosa, 2015). Although most older people will engage in learning for expressive reasons, the demands for workplace learning/education for older workers will continue to increase (Beatty & Visser, 2005). In addition, tertiary education providers need to expand their horizons to more readily embrace older people as lifelong learners in formal education.

The field of later life learning continues to grow exponentially and develop fresh perspectives as issues for older people gain more societal prominence. Whereas it is nearly always a governmental approach to give lip service to the importance of older adults' *learning* (because it is perceived that it is the individual's responsibility to choose what to learn), the *educational provision* for seniors remains much more problematic.

Suggested Cross-References

For more information on concepts and ideas discussed in this article, please see the following articles in the compendium: 1, 10, 12, 19, 52, 57, 61, 70, 74, 80

References

Aldridge, F., & Lavender, P. (2000). *The impact of learning on health*. Leicester, UK: National Institute of Adult Continuing Education.

Battersby, D. (1987). From andragogy to geragogy. *Journal of Educational Gerontology, 2*(1), 4–10.

Beatty, P. T., & Visser, R. M. S. (Eds.). (2005). *Thriving on an aging workforce: Strategies for organizational and systematic change*. Malabar, FL: Krieger.
Boulton-Lewis, G., & Tam, M. (Eds.). (2012). *Active ageing, active learning: Issues and challenges*. New York, NY: Springer International Publishing Switzerland.
Field, J. (2003). *Social capital*. London, England: Routledge.
Findsen, B. (2005). *Learning later*. Malabar, FL: Kreiger.
Findsen, B., & Formosa, M. (2011). *Lifelong learning in later life: A handbook on older adult learning*. Rotterdam, The Netherlands: Sense Publishers.
Findsen, B., & Formosa, M. (Eds.). (2016). *International perspectives on older adult education: Research, policy and practice*. New York, NY: Springer International Publishing Switzerland.
Formosa, M. (2000). Older adult education in a Maltese university of the third age: A critical perspective. *Education and Society, 15*(3), 315–339.
Formosa, M. (2015). *Ageing and later life in Malta: Issues, policies and future trends*. Valletta, Malta: International Institute on Ageing, United Nations.
Formosa, M., & Higgs, P. (Eds.). (2013). *Social class in later life: Power, identity and lifestyle*. Bristol, UK: Policy Press.
Glendenning, F. (Ed.). (2000). *Teaching and learning in later life: Theoretical implications*. Brookfield, VT: Ashgate Publishing Company.
Jarvis, P. (2001). *Learning in later life: An introduction for educators and carers*. London, England: Kogan Page.
Laslett, P. (1991). *A fresh map of life: The emergence of the third age* (Revised ed.). Cambridge, MA: Harvard University Press.
McClusky, H. Y. (1974). Education for aging: The scope of the field and perspectives for the future. *Learning for Aging*, 324–355.
Neugarten, B. (1976). Time, age and the life cycle. *American Journal of Psychiatry, 136*, 887–893.
Newman, S., & Hatton-Yeo, A. (2008). Intergenerational learning and the contributions of older people. *Ageing Horizons, 8*, 31–39.
Phillipson, C. (1998). *Reconstructing old age: New agendas in social theory and practice*. London, England: SAGE.
Phillipson, C. (2013). *Ageing*. Cambridge, UK: Polity Press.
Schmidt-Hertha, B., Kravosec, S. B., & Formosa, M. (Eds.). (2014). *Learning across generations in Europe: Contemporary issues in older adult education*. Rotterdam, The Netherlands: Sense.
Tuckett, A., & McAulay, A. (2005). *Demography and older learners: Approaches to a new policy challenge*. Leicester, UK: National Institute of Adult Continuing Education.
Withnall, A. (2010). *Improving learning in later life*. London, England: Routledge.

SECTION TWO

LEARNING THEORY AND PRACTICE

Articles in this section focus on explanations of the adult learning process, which reflects variations in capabilities, culture, brain-function, preparation, assumptions, and interests.

6

TRANSFORMATIVE LEARNING THEORY

Edward W. Taylor and Patricia Cranton

Keywords: change, learning theory, transformative learning

As a theory of change, transformative learning conceptualizes a significant shift in perspective during which an individual's perspective becomes more open, clarified, and supported (Cranton, 2016; Mezirow, 2000). Typically, transformative learning occurs when a person, group, or larger social unit encounters a perspective that is discrepant from the prevailing perspective. The discrepant perspective (e.g., personal event to a social movement) can't be ignored, and it fosters an examination of previously held beliefs, values, and assumptions.

Mezirow's (1991, 2000) view of transformative learning is the dominant conceptualization, where the unit of analysis is individual change. It reflects a predominantly rational approach emphasizing a critical and objective analysis of an interpretation of prior experience. Based to some extent on Habermas's (1971) communicative theory (e.g., instrumental, communicative learning), it recognizes that there is an innate drive among all humans to understand and make meaning of their experiences. Transformative learning rests on the assumption that there are no fixed truths and change is continuous, individuals cannot always be sure of what they know or believe, and it becomes imperative they continually explore ways to better understand their world by developing a more critical worldview. There is an inherent need for adults to better understand "how to negotiate and act on our own purposes, values, feelings, and meanings rather than those we have uncritically assimilated from others—to gain greater control over all lives as socially responsible clear thinking decision makers" (Mezirow, 2000, p. 8). Developing more reliable assumptions about the world, exploring and validating their dependability through critical reflection, and making decisions on an informed basis are seen as central to the adult learning process. The theory of transformation is seen as a psychocritical process of constructing and appropriating new or revised interpretations and assumptions of the meaning of an individual's experience (Mezirow, 2000).

This process is based on the assumption that each person has a worldview, a frame of reference, which is a collection of meaning structures of assumptions and expectations about their world that act as filters when interpreting experience (prior, new). It is the revision of a frame of reference initiated by a challenging experience, often referred to as a disorienting dilemma, that provokes an individual to critically reflect on prior experience potentially leading to a perspective transformation—"a more fully developed (more functional) frame of reference . . . one that is more (a) inclusive, (b) differentiating, (c) permeable, (d) critically reflective, and (e) integrative of experience" (Mezirow, 1996, p. 163). An outcome of this change is a sense of greater personal autonomy associated with a more authentic self "characterized by agency, choice, reflection, and rationality" (Tennant, 2012, p. 35).

In contrast to Mezirow's conception is an extrarational interpretation of transformative learning, which recognizes the limits of rationality and emphasizes the role imagination, intuition, and emotion (Dirkx, 2001). This conception is rooted in a Jungian theoretical framework of making sense of change, describing how symbols, images, and archetypes play a role in personal discernment and illumination as individuals work with unconscious issues in their life (Dirkx, 1998, 2001). Discernment, rather than reflection, is the central process of transformation that leads to personal enlightenment as individuals work to bring the unconscious to consciousness. We enter into a conscious relationship with images as we discover who we are as separate from and the same as others. A transformation from this perspective of transformative learning is seen as "a fundamental change in one's personality involving conjointly the resolution of a personal dilemma and the expansion of consciousness resulting in greater personality integration" (Boyd, 1991, p. 459). This process is an inner journey of individuation (Jung, [1921] 1971), with transformative learning conceptualized as an imaginative, intuitive, emotional, and soulful experience (Dirkx, 2006).

Another broad conception of transformative learning is social transformation (nonpsychological), which is a view of change that "is contextualized in the history, culture, and social fabric of the society in which he/she lives . . . at the intersection of the personal biography and societal structure"

(Cunningham, 1998, p. 16). This perspective (Brookfield, 2009; Freire, 1970) emphasizes ideological critique, dialogue, unveiling oppression, and social action in the context of transformative learning. As a theory or existence, an "ontological vocation" (Freire, 1970, p. 12), it views people as subjects, not objects, who are constantly reflecting and acting on the transformation of their world so it can become a more equitable place for all to live. It reflects a shift in the unit of analysis from the individual to the individual within the context of society, where the transformation of the individual and society are one and the same.

International Perspectives

The majority of the research and theoretical development on transformative learning has largely been a byproduct of scholars from North America, and it continues to be so. However, despite this trend there is a growing interest in transformative learning from an international perspective. Recently, for example, Kokkos (2012) conducted a review of work by European scholars involving transformative learning theory and found that most efforts were not about testing the theory, but more about using the theory to give meaning to learning of adults in general and in relationship to social change. Also revealed was that many European scholars were highly critical of Mezirow's conception, because "his approach has a strong cognitive emphasis" (p. 296) and neglects the affective, social, relational, and collective dimensions of learning. European researchers theoretically tend to draw on scholars who come from critical and social dimensions of learning (e.g., Bourdieu, Foucault, Giroux, Horkeimer, Engeström) as they make sense of transformative learning. A recent effort worth noting is a new theoretical conception of transformative learning rooted in assumptions of identity development from Denmark (Illeris, 2015), proactive insights into critical reflection and disorienting dilemmas from Finland (Mälkki, 2010, 2012), and a revised view of phases of transformative learning from Germany (Nohl, 2015).

Interestingly, there hasn't been much interest in exploring differences in transformative learning based on cultural differences (nationality, ethnicity). What little interest there is has been found in non-Western countries such as Africa where there is some effort at identifying cultural differences in the transformative process. Outcomes have been revealed that Africans, when learning, value "a unity of the spirit, mind, and body," "wisdom over formal knowledge," the important role of proverbs (Ntseane, 2012, p. 285), and an appreciation for community-based approaches to transformative learning (Mejiuni, 2012).

When reviewing specific research studies about transformative learning in other cultures besides the United States, Taylor (2012) found an emerging body of work "that originates in almost all the major continents of the world" (p. 43). Unfortunately, only a few studies made an effort at exploring cultural differences and transformative learning (e.g., Duveskog, Friis-Hansen, & Taylor, 2011; Merriam & Ntseane, 2008; Moyer, Sinclair, & Diduck, 2014; Sims & Sinclair, 2008). Despite the scarcity of scholarship on transformative learning from an international perspective, research is starting to reveal that there are both differences between cultures (e.g., presentational knowing) and universal aspects (e.g., role of relationships) within the process of transformative learning.

Fostering Transformative Learning in Practice

Over time, transformative learning has also become a framework for teaching adults in formal and nonformal settings. Fostering change within an educational setting is about helping

> learners move from a simple awareness of their experiencing to an awareness of the conditions for their experiencing (how they are perceiving, thinking, judging, feeling, acting—a reflection on process) and beyond this to an awareness of the reasons why they experience as they do and to action based upon these insights. (Mezirow, 1991, p. 197)

Originally, three interrelated components were identified as central to the process of transformative learning: the centrality of experience, critical reflection, and dialogue. Individual experience comprises the practical knowledge, skill, and understanding of the world that every adult brings into the classroom. Experience "constitutes a starting point for discourse leading to critical examination of normative assumptions underpinning the learner's . . . value judgments or normative expectations" (Mezirow, 2000, p. 3). Critical reflection, the questioning and revising of deeply held assumptions in dialogue with others and the self, relies on the person being exposed to a variety of points of view or perspectives that are discrepant with those currently held (provoking what Mezirow refers to as a disorienting dilemma). Dialogue creates conditions that support and provoke critical self-reflection. Some strategies found in different settings include the following: using controversial readings and readings from different points of view, giving group members responsibility for monitoring and controlling the direction of the discourse to ensure equal participation without coercion, and being aware of the educator's power to shape dialogue through verbal and nonverbal communication (Cranton, 2016).

However, through extensive research other essential elements of practice have been identified (Taylor, 2007, 2014; Mezirow, Taylor, & Associates, 2009) that can be collapsed into three broad elements. They include a holistic orientation, awareness of context, and engaging in an authentic practice. The first element is a holistic orientation, which encourages the "engagement with music, all the plastic arts, dance, movement, and mime, as well as all forms of myth, fable, allegory, and drama" (Davis-Manigualte, Yorks, & Kasl, 2006, p. 27) and an appreciation for the role of the affective and relational in fostering change (Mezirow et al., 2009). By engaging the affective it provides a means to address the dynamics associated with a resistance to learning, as well as potentially initiating a process of individuation, that of "a deeper understanding, realization, and appreciation of who he or she is" (p. 18). A second element is the importance of developing an awareness of the personal and sociocultural factors that influence transformative learning. These factors include the surroundings within the immediate learning event occurring in the classroom, the prior life history of the participants, and the larger societal events that are playing out in society. A third element for fostering change includes the importance of supportive and meaningful relationships among people that are based on authenticity—the educator bringing a genuine sense of self into the classroom and working to help learners become authentic in their interactions with the educator and others (Palmer, 2008). It requires a perspective that reflects love for the world and human beings, humility, faith in people, hope that the dialogue will lead to meaning, and critical thinking and the continuing transformation of reality (Freire, 1970). A fourth element that is often overlooked is that of empathy. Empathy provides a framework for understanding the role of emotions in relationship to critical reflection, the means to inform practice in more effectively fostering critical reflection, and offers a more sophisticated understanding of the outcomes of transformative learning theory (Taylor, 2014).

These elements are not a group of teaching strategies that are applied arbitrarily; they are general principles interrelated and theoretically grounded in deeply held assumptions about the transformative nature of adult learning. To engage in the application of these core elements without some awareness of transformative learning would be indicative of teaching without a clear purpose or goal.

Conclusion

In North America, transformative learning theory is presently the most comprehensive theory of adult learning, and it is rapidly gaining the interest of scholars in Europe, Asia, and Africa. Transformative learning is a deep shift in perspective during which a worldview becomes more open, more permeable, and better justified. This shift occurs through reflection, imagination, intuition, emotion, and engaging with symbols and myths. It can be an individual process, a group process, and a process of social change. Transformative learning is seen as unique to adulthood, especially the rational perspective that requires a sense of metacognition, which is not fully developed until adulthood (Merriam, 2004). However, it is not always clear how transformative learning differs from deep learning, active learning, relational learning, and the like. It has a constructivist foundation, as do many other learning theories, and there is considerable overlap between the characteristics of transformative learning and more general learning theories.

Several perspectives on transformative learning theory have evolved over the decades since Mezirow first presented his concept of "perspective transformation" in the 1970s. Following the first wave of theoretical development in which authors critiqued and expanded on Mezirow's work, a second wave of theoretical development focuses on integrative and holistic understandings of the theory. In this article, we provided an overview of three broad perspectives, an international perspective, as well as a view of the practice of fostering transformative learning with the intent to offer an inclusive portrayal of the field. Less has been written about fostering transformative learning, but this is changing with, for example, Mezirow and colleagues' (2009) book and Hogan, Simpson, and Stuckey's (2009) collection of ways to incorporate creative expression to promote transformation.

Suggested Cross-References

For more information on concepts and ideas discussed in this article, please see the following articles in the compendium: 1, 2, 4, 5, 7, 10, 11, 12, 14, 19, 23, 25, 28, 34, 35, 39, 41, 51, 52, 56, 57, 58, 65, 66, 70, 74, 78, 79, 80

References

Boyd, R. D. (1991). *Personal transformation in small groups: A Jungian perspective.* London, England: Routledge.

Brookfield, S. (2009). Engaging critical reflection in corporate America. In J. Mezirow & E. W. Taylor (Eds.), *Transformative learning in practice* (pp. 125–135). San Francisco, CA: Jossey-Bass.

Cranton, P. (2016). *Understanding and promoting transformative learning* (2nd ed.) Sterling, VA: Stylus.

Cunningham, P. M. (1998). The social dimension of transformative learning. *Pennsylavania Association for Adult Continuing Education Journal of Lifelong Learning, 7*, 15–28.

Davis-Manigualte, J., Yorks, L., & Kasl, E. (2006). Expressive ways of knowing and transformative learning. In E. W. Taylor (Ed.), *Teaching for change* (No. 109; pp. 27–35). San Francisco: Jossey-Bass.

Dirkx, J. (1998). Transformative learning theory in the practice of adult education: An overview. *Pennsylavania Association for Adult Continuing Education Journal of Lifelong Learning, 7*, 1–14.

Dirkx, J. (2001). Images, transformative learning and the work of soul. *Adult Learning, 12*(3), 15–16.

Dirkx, J. (2006). Engaging emotions in adult learning: A Jungian perspective on emotion and transformative learning. In E. W. Taylor (Ed.), *Teaching for change: Fostering transformative learning in the classroom* (No. 109; pp. 15–26). New Directions for Adult and Continuing Education. San Francisco: Jossey-Bass.

Duveskog, D., Friis-Hansen, E., & Taylor, E. W. (2011). Farmer-field schools in rural Kenya: A transformative learning experience. *Journal of Development.* Retrieved from http://dx.doi.org/10.1080/00220388.2011.561328

Freire, P. (1970). *Pedagogy of the oppressed.* New York, NY: Continuum.

Habermas, J. (1971). *Knowledge and human interests.* Boston, MA: Beacon Press.

Hogan, C., Simpson, S., & Stuckey, H. (Eds.). (2009). Creative expression in transformative learning: Tools and techniques for educators of adults. Malabar, FL: Krieger.

Illeris, K. (2015). Transformative learning and identity. *Journal of Transformative Education, 12*(2), 148–163.

Jung, C. (1971, originally published in 1921). *Psychological types.* Princeton, NJ: Princeton University Press.

Kokkos, A. (2012). Transformative learning in Europe: An overview of the theoretical perspectives. In E. Taylor & P. Cranton (Eds.), *Handbook of transformative learning theory: Theory, research and practice* (pp. 289–303). San Francisco, CA: Jossey-Bass.

Mälkki, K. (2010). Building on Mezirow's theory of transformative learning: Theorizing the challenges to reflection. *Journal of Transformative Education, 8*(1), 42–62.

Mälkki, K. (2012). Rethinking disorienting dilemmas within real-life crisis: The role of reflection in negotiating emotionally chaotic experiences. *Adult Education Quarterly, 62*(3), 207–229.

Mejiuni, O. (2012). International and community-based transformative learning. In E. Taylor & P. Cranton (Eds.), *Handbook of transformative learning theory: Theory, research and practice* (pp. 304–319). San Francisco, CA: Jossey-Bass.

Merriam, S. B. (2004). The role of cognitive development in Mezirow's transformational learning theory. *Adult Education Quarterly: A Journal of Research and Theory, 55*(1), 60–68.

Merriam, S. B., & Ntseane, P. G. (2008). Transformational learning in Botswana: How culture shapes the process. *Adult Education Quarterly, 58*(3), 183–197.

Mezirow, J. (1991). *Transformative dimensions of adult learning.* San Francisco, CA: Jossey-Bass.

Mezirow, J. (1996). Contemporary paradigms of learning. *Adult Education Quarterly, 46*, 158–172.

Mezirow, J. (2000). Transformative learning. In J. Mezirow & Associates (Eds.), *Learning as transformation* (pp. 1–33). San Francisco, CA: Jossey-Bass.

Mezirow, J., Taylor, E. W., & Associates (Eds.). (2009). *The practice of fostering transformative learning.* San Francisco, CA: Jossey-Bass.

Moyer, J. M., Sinclair, J. A., & Diduck, A. P. (2014). Learning for sustainability among faith-based organizations in Kenya. *Environmental Management, 54*(2), 360–372.

Nohl, A. M. (2015). Typical phases of transformative learning: A practice based model. *Adult Education Quarterly, 65*(1), 35–49.

Ntseane, P. G. (2012). Transformative learning theory: A perspective from Africa. In E. W. Taylor & P. Cranton (Eds.), *Handbook of transformative learning theory: Theory, research and practice* (pp. 274–288). San Francisco, CA: Jossey-Bass.

Palmer, P. (2008). *The courage to teach: Exploring the inner landscape of a teacher's life.* San Francisco, CA: Jossey-Bass.

Sims, L., & Sinclair, A. J. (2008). Learning through participatory resource management programs: Case studies in Costa Rica. *Adult Education Quarterly, 58*(2), 151–168.

Taylor, E. W. (2007). An update of transformative learning theory: A critical review of the empirical research (1999–2005). *International Journal of Lifelong Education, 26*, 173–191.

Taylor, E. W. (2012). A critical review of research on transformative learning theory, 2006–2010. In E. Taylor & P. Cranton (Eds.), *Handbook of transformative learning theory: Theory, research and practice* (pp. 37–55). San Francisco, CA: Jossey-Bass.

Taylor, E. W. (2014/2015). Empathy: The stepchild of critical reflection and transformative learning. *Educational Reflective Practices, 4*(2), 5–24.

Tennant, M. (2012). *The learning self.* San Francisco, CA: Jossey-Bass.

7

THE RELEVANCE OF INDIGENOUS KNOWLEDGE FOR ADULT EDUCATION

Sandra L. Morrison and Timote Vaioleti

Keywords: adult education, assessment, change, community, engaged, ethnographic, indigenous adult education, indigenous education, indigenous knowledge, individual perspective, renewal

Over generations, indigenous peoples across the world have built up layers and layers of complex history and knowledge that connects them with their environment, their spiritual world, and their ancestors and allows them to live sustainably and wisely for the well-being of their collectives. These knowledge systems came from observation and experience and were often tested against natural and human phenomena (Thaman, 2009). Despite the onslaught of systemic colonization, indigenous knowledge systems still exist. Some are vibrant and dynamic, adjusting to a rapidly changing technological world and others, depending on the context, struggle to stay intact. Even so, in many parts of the world an indigenous knowledge system quite different than a Western knowledge system has been regenerating and informing indigenous communities as they go about their daily lives and informing other social systems such as education.

This article explores the value of indigenous adult education and its contribution in making education relevant in the twenty-first century. It looks at initiatives for cultural renewal with examples from the New Zealand Māori adult education experiences. This article discusses the relevance of indigenous adult education for nonindigenous communities.

Understanding the Term *Indigenous*

It is always difficult to arrive at one definition that is relevant to the many contexts and circumstances that indigenous people experience. Nevertheless, the International Work Group for Indigenous Affairs (n.d.) has come up with a modern understanding of the term based on the following factors:

- Self-identification as indigenous peoples at the individual level and accepted by the community as their member
- Historical continuity with precolonial and/or presettler societies
- A strong connection to territories and surrounding natural resources
- Distinct social, economic, or political systems
- Distinct language, culture, and beliefs
- Formation of nondominant groups of society
- Resolve to maintain and reproduce ancestral environments and systems as distinctive peoples and communities

This understanding, however, does not take into consideration those cultures that are the majority grouping in their country. For example, some countries in the South Pacific such as Tonga, Samoa, Kiribati, and the Solomon Islands regard themselves as indigenous and remain the dominant group in their own countries, contrary to the understanding mentioned earlier. What seems to be the defining quality and foremost in the thinking by indigenous people is their tie to land. Many indigenous people prefer to self-define with key reference to their tribe, village, or island, not accepting an outsider's imposed definition. For instance, many Māori will articulate primarily the name of their tribe and their tribe's territorial indicators as identifying factors of who they are, as illustrated in the following examples:

- Ko Ngongotaha te maunga
- Ko Rotorua te moana
- Ko Tamatekapua te tangata
- Ko Te Arawa te iwi
- My mountain is called Ngongotaha
- My lake is called Rotorua
- My leader is called Tamatekapua
- My tribe is Te Arawa

Like many other indigenous peoples, Māori are place-based people and identify themselves with the features of their place, surrounding landscapes, system of values, beliefs, and symbolic representations of their world.

Adult Education

The intervention of the debilitating power of colonization was an obvious interruption to the advancement of indigenous knowledge systems. Against an education system that was antagonistic to their needs and whose epistemological basis was generally based on a value system far removed from their own realities, indigenous people struggled to learn, resulting even today in a disproportionate number of indigenous people featuring in negative social indices such as education. Many indigenous peoples entering into adult education today are second-chance learners.

Traditionally, education for indigenous peoples was seamless and was to benefit the well-being of the collective who usually lived together in their kin groups and with constant connection and dependence on their lands. Learning was purposeful and aimed at the acquisition of skills and knowledge to perform inherited roles dictated by the collective (Vaioleti, 2011; Vaioleti & Morrison, 2015).

Intergenerational transfer of knowledge was inherent in this philosophical approach to education and occurred through osmosis, observation, informal learning, and nonformal learning, including apprenticeship. John Rangihau (1975) writes: "My education as a Māori was a matter of observation while I grew up in this complete community" (p. 223). *Complete community* then refers to a community that is self-sustaining, self-determining, and whose education was designed around achieving good relationships with each other and the environment.

With over 5,000 different indigenous and tribal groups in the world, comprising approximately 370 million people, the diversity amid indigenous variation must be contextualized to their country, region, and colonizing experience. There is also no one way of being indigenous. Diverse realities exist and many indigenous people, as with other societal groupings, now live away from their tribal territories (International Work Group for Indigenous Affairs, n.d.).

Despite their diversity, there are some commonalities, experiences, and a shared value system common to most indigenous peoples. At the heart of indigenous identity is the distinctiveness of collective groupings who embrace the spiritual world. They are bound together by kinship, language, history, cooperation, reciprocity, and a strong sense of place (Maaka & Anderson, 2006). All indigenous education has this relational and holistic goal in one form or another (Vaioleti, 2011).

Benefit of Adult Education

Adult education differs from formal education as it is problem-based, primarily designed to deal with current issues, often concerned with justice. In some developed countries, nation-states are addressing and reconciling their actions of colonial oppressions through settlement processes, and in recent years nation-states have assumed the responsibility of providing resources and facilities for indigenous education, albeit not without reticence and hesitation (Stavenhagen, 1998). Still, this has supported redesigning institutions in order to respond more positively to the aspirations of indigenous peoples, particularly in the social sectors, including education.

There are excellent models of Māori-centered formal educational initiatives across the age spectrum and examples of adult education initiatives. Tribal universities that have a Māori philosophical base allow students to learn from a Māori epistemological base and in their own language. Tribal authorities have a commitment to ensuring the continuation of their tribal knowledge and language and invest heavily in a range of formal and nonformal programs to build tribal capacity across many disciplines. Learning takes place according to Māori pedagogy and is often held in the traditional meeting houses. Traditional ceremonies and rituals are all part of the learning process in what Battiste (2002) explains as the spirit connecting processes that enable the gift, visions, and spirits to emerge in each person. Learning is a living process.

The Relevance of Indigenous Adult Education to Wider Society

Coates (2004) states that indigenous societies find themselves torn between the localizing power of their cultures and the unifying forces of the contemporary world. Indeed the biggest challenge for indigenous adult education is how to prepare people to live in a changing world and still maintain traditional systems of knowledge. The identification of core principles and values that indigenous communities view as critical to meeting their own political, environmental, economic, and social development is essential.

Indigenous peoples must be at the fore of making decisions about advancing their own education that line up with their aspirations. Education policy largely has intentionally and unintentionally contributed to invalidating indigenous peoples' knowledge systems, and decisions have been made without indigenous people at the decision-making table. To achieve buy-in and success and increase participation in adult education systems, their leadership is necessary. Further, there should be an effort to work with the cultural potential that indigenous people bring to the table rather than follow the deficit model that has plagued their involvement in education for far too long. What is good for indigenous people must surely be good for all if individual and community empowerment is to be raised.

With indigenous peoples living among majority populations, there is a growing call for an intercultural bilingual education that is rooted in one's own culture, language, values, worldview, and system of knowledge but, at the same time, is receptive of, open to, and appreciative of others' knowledge (UNESCO, 2009). For young people and adults whose experience in the formal sector may have been negative, pathways into adult education can be facilitated through indigenous systems with access to culturally relevant programs that build knowledge and skills necessary to function fully as an effective member of both their own community and mainstream society. This principle of active citizenship is important in helping build cohesive societies and reducing inequalities.

An indigenous adult education model also offers alternative worldviews. With environmental constraints becoming part of global concerns such as climate change and disaster risk prevention, societies are becoming more willing to engage with alternative worldviews realizing the limitations of a monocultural education system. If indigenous knowledge, especially that knowledge held by traditional knowledge bearers (generally elders) is valued in the same way that the sciences are valued, then working in the interface of both knowledge systems can only bring mutual advantages, especially in enhancing an ethic of care for the planet and for people. This same model can also be applied in many other areas, such as technological advancement.

Conclusion

Indigenous adult education systems elevate indigenous people to engage and participate in their own society and the wider society at a much more sophisticated level than if they did not exist. With robust systems of adaptability and resilience, indigenous people continue to offer an alternative perspective to their place in the world. Central to their worldview is the importance of relationships and people, a conscious reminder to mainstream societies who seek to find sustainable and peaceful solutions to an ever-changing complex and challenging world.

Suggested Cross-References

For more information on concepts and ideas discussed in this article, please see the following articles in the compendium: 6, 11, 14, 19, 22, 35, 42, 52, 57, 64, 65, 69, 70, 71, 76, 79, 80

References

Battiste, M. (2002). *Indigenous knowledge and pedagogy in First Nations education: A literature review with recommendations.* Prepared for National Working Group on Education and the Minister of Indian Affairs. Indian and Northern Affairs, Ottawa, Canada.

Coates, S. (2004). *A global history of indigenous peoples, struggle and survival.* New York, NY: Palgrave.

International Work Group for Indigenous Affairs. (n.d.). Retrieved from http://www.iwgia.org/culture-and-identity/identification-of-indigenous-peoples

Maaka, R. C. A., & Andersen, C. (2006). *The indigenous experience, global perspectives.* Toronto, Canada: Canadian Scholars' Press.

Rangihau, J. (1975). Being Maori. In M. King (Eds.), *Te ao hurihuri, the world moves on. Aspects of Maoritanga* (pp. 221–233). Wellington, NZ: Hicks Smith & Sons.

Stavenhagen, R. (1998). Indigenous people and adult education: A growing challenge. In L. King (Ed.), *Reflecting visions: New perspectives on adult education for indigenous peoples* (pp. 1–3). Lanham, MD: UNESCO Institute for Education.

Thaman, K. (2009). Making the good things last. A vision of education for peace and sustainable development in the Asia Pacific region. Retrieved from http://www.accu.or.jp/esd/forum_esd_2009/pdf/fji_kon.pdf

UNESCO. (2009). *UNESCO World Report. Investing in cultural diversity and intercultural dialogue.* Paris, France: UNESCO.

Vaioleti, T. M. (2011). *Talanoa, Manulua and Founga Ako: Frameworks for using enduring Tongan educational ideas for education in Aotearoa/New Zealand.* (Doctoral Dissertation, University of Waikato, Hamilton, NZ).

Vaioleti, T. M., & Morrison, S. L. (2015). Traditional concepts for Māori and Pacific adult education and lifelong learning. *International Perspectives in Adult Education, 71*, 220–228.

8

THE COGNITIVE ASPECT OF ADULT LEARNERS FROM NEUROSCIENCE

Wei-Wen Chang

Keywords: abilities, adaptation, adult education, adult learner, attitudes, autonomy, change, contexts, empathy, engaged, evaluation, experience, experiential, interdisciplinary, learning, observation, performance, reflection, resistance, social, unlearning

Technological advancement has enhanced the development of imaging studies in neuroscience. Scientific studies provide new information regarding how the human mind works in a biological perspective, whereas how to connect these studies with learning theories and apply them in educational practice relies on cross-field dialogues and collaboration. This article, from an interdisciplinary perspective, examines three issues in adult education—experiential learning, social learning, and learning for change—with information from recent cognitive neuroscience. This review indicates the need for constant collaboration between education and neuroscience for more circumspect applications.

Change is constant and continuing education becomes critical for people who must address change. In past decades, researchers portrayed the characteristics of adult learners through various learning models or theories such as the experiential learning model or social learning theory (Gallese, Fadiga, Fogassi, & Rizzolatti, 1996; Kolb, 2015). The development of brain research has also helped reveal underlying reasons for certain learning behaviors

(Chiao & Ambady, 2007). Research in both fields continually extends our understanding of adult learners. Through an interdisciplinary perspective, this article discusses (a) neuroplasticity and experiential learning, (b) mirror neurons and social learning, and (c) neural automaticity and learning for change. Under each issue, scientific findings and their relevance to adult education are discussed.

Neuroimaging Studies on Adult Learners

Various neuroimaging studies have been conducted on adult learners focusing on neuroplasticity, mirror neurons, and neural automicity.

Neuroplasticity and Experiential Learning

Decades ago, medical researchers found that the brain has the plasticity to repair itself and that individuals' external experiences are associated with structural changes in the brain; hence, neuroplasticity is related to learning (Draganski et al., 2004; Eriksson et al., 1998). For example, Maguire and colleagues (2000) found that, with more navigation experience in their jobs, taxi drivers' posterior hippocampi (an area associated with spatial processing) were significantly larger than those of control subjects. The volume correlated positively with the length of time spent as a taxi driver. This indicates that environmental enrichment and repeated exercise increases neuron generation.

Experience and learning are intertwined. Individuals experience an event, reflect on the experience, and may change future actions based on the reflection (Kolb, 2015). As a result of brain research, we now know that these experiences change the brain (Gage, 2004) even in adulthood. This indicates the importance of *repetition* in designing learning experiences. Repetition design has been widely used for skill training, such as learning to ride a bicycle. However, for training that involves social interactions, such as leadership development or crisis management, creating repeated experiences is challenging because each incident is grounded in a unique context and therefore cannot be duplicated.

Although it has been proven that exposure to experience is related to learning, the level of involvement in such exposure also affects how much change will occur. For example, Chang and Yuan (2013) discussed the relationship between people's international experience and cross-cultural adaptability. One group was deeply involved in the culture and the second group stayed on the fringes. Statistical results showed that the adaptability of the high-involvement group was significantly higher than that of the low-involvement group. This study indicates that even though neurons have the plasticity to learn from experience, the external level of involvement affects the internal development.

Mirror Neurons and Social Learning

Learning is seen through not only the individual but also the social. Bandura (1971) knew that individuals learned behaviors by watching others, and now we know the brain's mirror neurons help in the social learning process (Gallese et al., 1996). Mirror neurons help explain how people learn through mimicry and why people can empathize with each other. The mirroring mechanism can activate the same brain cells whether by first-person execution or third-person observation of an action. These cells have a profound effect on social cognition, especially in recognizing emotions and interpreting nonverbal actions (Molnar-Szakacs, Wu, Robles, & Iacoboni, 2007).

In short, mirror neurons provide biological support for social learning theory. This not only explains how we learn from others but also reveals an extensive learning network in which everyone is connected and has influence on each other. This has important implications for workplace learning in organizations. Leaders' emotions and actions prompt team members to mirror these feelings and deeds, and the effect of activating neural circuitry in the followers' brains can be powerful (Goleman & Boyatzis, 2008). Barsade (2002) used the term *ripple effect* to describe the prevalent and immediate influence of emotional contagion on group behavior. In other words, a leader's development consciously or unconsciously affects the growth of his or her subordinates and vice versa. Because of the natural effect of mirror neurons, the development of leaders and employees do not stand independently; rather, they are strongly and closely intertwined. Whereas neural mirroring shows that individuals are predisposed to others' behavior, neural automaticity shows that repeated experience causes the same patterns in the brain (Maguire et al., 2000; Waytz & Mason, 2013). Although this is an efficient way for the brain to work, it may inhibit change.

Neural Automaticity and Learning for Change

According to the experiential learning model, behavior is an accumulation of lifelong experiences (Kolb, 2015). While the experience was being repeated frequently, a stable framework was gradually being established. Such stable frameworks help people respond to similar situations better, but this mechanism may in turn become an obstacle to making changes. Recent scientific studies show that repeated experiences and behaviors increase neuron automaticity, thus requiring less reasoning and mental effort. Neuroscientists Waytz and Mason (2013) noted that incoming sensory information is transmitted to the affected brain network via two routes. The first is an expressway that bypasses brain areas that support conscious reasoning (neural automaticity); the other is the local road that runs through more brain regions to the affected network. The expressway involves fewer brain regions and requires less energy. Neural automaticity lets people respond to a familiar stimulus more quickly with less effort. People's behaviors, including change, involve economic choices. According to the *law of least effort*, people try to use the least effort necessary to reach the same goal (Kahneman, 2011).

During adulthood, people inevitably face new challenges that cannot be solved by the existing model. Learning how to adjust and change, behaviorally and mentally, becomes one of the major purposes of continuing education. However, an established expressway requiring less effort may become the root of resistance to change because changes require people to give up their familiar expressway and rebuild a new path initially having a higher energy cost (Waytz & Mason, 2013). In many instances, people attempt to make changes, but the neural automaticity unconsciously drives them back to their habitual behaviors or thinking patterns. As Hislop, Bosley, Coombs, and Holland (2014) suggest, change involves not only acquiring new knowledge but also giving up or abandoning some established knowledge, thinking patterns, or behaviors, that is, unlearning. However, how to accomplish change or unlearning is still a struggle for many educators, and even for the learners themselves, because when people face the choice of old and new patterns, the choice requiring less effort (the old pattern) often seems the more appealing of the two.

With an understanding of this aspect of our biological nature, researchers have tried to examine whether people may be able to pause automatic thinking routes and increase mental strength to manage work, life, and oneself. To achieve such purposes, since 2006 executive master of business administration (EMBA) programs throughout Asia have used a learning activity known as the Gobi Desert Challenge. This annual competition, held in a large desert region, attracts thousands of EMBA students hoping to strengthen their psychical endurance and determination (National University of Singapore, 2014). Three components are included in the learning design:

1. The special nature of the environment: The Gobi Desert is the fifth largest desert in the world and the largest in Asia, and has extreme temperatures ranging from 50° C (122° F) to –40° C (–40° F). The road is harsh; the weather is dry and windy. During the competition, people live in a camp and must finish a 112-km trek (approximately 70 miles) within 4 days.

2. Inspiring spirit: Approximately 1,300 years ago, a monk named Xuangzang walked through the Gobi alone toward India with a strong determination to search for the Buddha's classic teaching and wisdom. When faced with a difficult choice of either taking the high risk of dying in the desert or returning to survive, he resolved to continue his journey. His strong will and perseverance has had a significant influence on Chinese culture and the propagation of Buddhism worldwide. In the competition, when participants want to give up, this inspiring legend encourages them to move forward.
3. Team support: Every individual must go through severe challenges. However, a team cannot claim to have completed the competition unless all its members have arrived at the end point.

EMBA students come to the Gobi to learn something not shown in textbooks. They learn to unlearn part of themselves. For adults, learning how to unlearn is critical for them to navigate through difficult challenges, creating a new path in preparation for their next stage. Through an understanding of neural automaticity, scientific studies have helped to portray the picture regarding the learning and unlearning process from a biological perspective, which in turn provides adult educators with new opportunities to reexamine conventional theories and program designs.

Conclusion

Recent imaging technology has significantly increased the growth of neuroscience, and many findings are highly related to education (Ames & Fiske, 2010). However, teachers are receiving numerous "brain-based learning" packages containing alarming amounts of misinformation (Goswami, 2006, p. 406). To more appropriately apply the scientific findings to educational fields in the future, collaboration from different disciplines is crucial in bridging the gap between science and practice. This article has reviewed three major findings in neuroscience—neuroplasticity, mirror neurons, and neural automaticity—and discussed their respective relevance to experiential learning, social learning, and learning for change. The implications of these studies suggest that as human behaviors constantly involve mental and biological factors, learning designers must be aware of the influence from both aspects, especially when learners face difficulties or resist moving further. The new findings in neuroscience continually update our understanding regarding the dynamic between external stimulus and internal neural structures, which helps provide more comprehensive insights on how learning or unlearning occurs. Teamwork from researchers in these two fields is critical to bridge the different foci and generate appropriate interventions for educational purposes. Through a dialogue between adult education and neuroscience, more understanding and collaborative opportunities can be identified and developed for learning enhancement.

Suggested Cross-References

For more information on concepts and ideas discussed in this article, please see the following articles in the compendium: 4, 6, 9, 11, 12, 13, 51, 58, 71, 72, 77, 78, 79

References

Ames, D. L., & Fiske, S. (2010). Cultural neuroscience. *Asian Journal of Social Psychology, 13,* 72–82.

Bandura, A. (1971). *Social learning theory.* New York, NY: General Learning Press.

Barsade, S. G. (2002). The ripple effect: Emotional contagion and its influence on group behavior. *Administrative Science Quarterly, 47,* 644–675.

Chang, W. W., & Yuan, Y. H. (2013). The relationship between international experience and cross-cultural adaptability. *International Journal of Intercultural Relations, 37*(2), 268–273.

Chiao, J. Y., & Ambady, N. (2007). Cultural neuroscience: Parsing universality and diversity across levels of analysis. In S. Kitayama & D. Cohen (Eds.), *Handbook of cultural psychology* (pp. 237–254). New York, NY: Guilford Press.

Draganski, B., Gaser, C., Busch, V., Schuierer, G., Bogdahn, U., & May, A. (2004). Neuroplasticity: Changes in grey matter induced by training. *Nature, 427,* 311–312.

Eriksson, P. S., Perfilieva, E., Björk-Eriksson, T., Alborn, A. M., Nordborg, C., Peterson, D. A., & Gage, F. H. (1998). Neurogenesis in the adult human hippocampus. *Nature Medicine, 4*(11), 1313–1317.

Gage, F. H. (2004). Structural plasticity of the adult brain. *Dialogues in Clinical Neuroscience, 6*(2), 135–141.

Gallese, V., Fadiga, L., Fogassi, L., & Rizzolatti, G. (1996). Action recognition in the premotor cortex. *Brain, 119*(2), 593–609.

Goleman, D., & Boyatzis, R. (2008). Social intelligence and the biology of leadership. *Harvard Business Review, 86*(9), 74–81.

Goswami, U. (2006). Neuroscience and education: From research to practice? *Nature Reviews Neuroscience, 7*(5), 406–411.

Hislop, D., Bosley, S., Coombs, C. R., & Holland, J. (2014). The process of individual unlearning: A neglected topic in an under-researched field. *Management Learning, 45*(5), 540–560.

Kahneman, D. (2011). *Thinking, fast and slow.* New York, NY: Farrar, Straus and Giroux.

Kolb, D. A. (2015). *Experiential learning: Experience as the source of learning and development.* Upper Saddle River, NJ: Pearson Education.

Maguire, E. A., Gadian, D. G., Johnsrude, I. S., Good, C. D., Ashburner, J., Frackowiak, R. S. J., & Frith, C. D. (2000). Navigation-related structural change in the hippocampi of taxi drivers. *Proceedings of the National Academy of Sciences of the United States of America, 97*, 4398–4403.

Molnar-Szakacs, I., Wu, A. D., Robles, F. J., & Iacoboni, M. (2007). Do you see what I mean? Corticospinal excitability during observation of culture-specific gestures. *Public Library of Science One, 2*(7), e626.

National University of Singapore. (2014). NUS business school takes on the Gobi desert challenge. Retrieved from http://gobichallenge.nus.edu/about-the-challenge/eng/

Waytz, A., & Mason, M. (2013). Your brain at work. *Harvard Business Review, 91*(7/8), 102–111.

9

ADULT LITERACY PRACTICES AND ADULT BASIC EDUCATION

M. Cecil Smith

Keywords: adult basic education, adult literacy, community, confidence, contexts, engaged, environment, evaluation, international, literacy practices, literacy skills, mentor, non-formal, numeracy, practices, problem-solving, proficiency, scaffolding, workplace learning

Adult basic and literacy education programs take many forms and adopt a variety of approaches to instruction. Around the globe, these programs range from formal, state-sponsored regimens that are driven by endorsed curricula and assessment protocols and administered by professional educators to informal programs that are led by volunteers, usually from local communities or neighborhoods. The scope and quality of the instruction provided often depend on a variety of factors, such as the guiding philosophy of the provider organization, the theories about learning that are endorsed by program directors, the training of the teachers and/or volunteers, the knowledge and skill levels of the adult learners on program entry, and the learners' collective and individual learning goals. The instruction found that adult basic education (ABE) literacy programs generally center on teaching functionally illiterate or low-literate adults how to read, write, and perform basic math functions or introducing them to personal computers. However, typically, there is greatest instructional emphasis on improving adults' reading skills (e.g., the ability to decode words and comprehend written texts) rather than writing or numeracy. A functionally illiterate individual is a person who lacks the reading, writing, and math skills to perform everyday tasks and manage daily living activities. Low-literate adults are those who can perform simple literacy tasks, but not more challenging ones; or, these persons may be literate in their native language but not in the majority language, such as English. In the United States, these individuals are referred to as English-as-a-Second Language (ESL) learners.

A recent international study in 40 countries assessed and compared the basic literacy skills, and a broad range of competencies, of adults ages 16 to 65. The Survey of Adult Skills is a component of the Program for the International Assessment of Adult Competencies (PIAAC; National Center for Education Statistics, n.d.), and its assessment protocol focuses on the cognitive and workplace skills deemed necessary for adults to fully participate in the global economy of twenty-first-century society. The survey measures adults' proficiencies in literacy, numeracy, and problem solving in technology-rich environments (e.g., the ability to use ICTs to locate, evaluate, and use information online), as well as the relationships between individuals' educational background, work skills and experiences, occupational attainment, and uses of information and communication technologies (ICTs). Approximately 250,000 adults were surveyed in the official language(s) of their native countries. In most of the participating countries, significant proportions of adults performed at lower proficiency levels on the literacy and numeracy measures: between 5% and 28% of adults demonstrated the lowest proficiency levels in literacy, and between 8% and 32% are only proficient at the lowest levels in numeracy. Further, large proportions of the population in many countries have no experience with, or lack the basic skills needed to use, ICTs for many everyday tasks (OECD, 2013). These results demonstrate the need in many countries around the world for ABE programs to improve adults' reading, writing, numeracy, and ICT skills.

Reading instruction for functionally illiterate and ESL adults may focus on letter-to-sound correspondence (decoding), vocabulary knowledge, reading speed (fluency), and comprehension. Instructional materials can include either commercially produced basal readers and skills workbooks or authentic reading materials that learners encounter in their everyday lives, such as periodicals, bills and forms, and books. Basal readers are sequenced, grade-level reading materials consisting of short narratives combined with skills exercises. Alternatively, instructors may employ a mix of commercial curricula and authentic text materials. Decisions about what kinds of instructional materials are appropriate for adult learners often depend upon program funders' or administrators' views of the nature and purposes of literacy.

The social contextual view of adult literacy holds that social and cultural variables determine individual literacy skills and practices. Literacy ability is not merely the application of a set of distinct, autonomous skills that can be readily transferred to any task or situation (Street, 1985). The social contexts of adults' lives largely determine the kinds of literacy practices in which adults engage (Smith, 1996), as these contexts create the conditions that may demand, improve, support, or undermine literacy skills and practices. Individuals participate in diverse literacy practices—reading, writing, numeracy, listening, speaking, using ICTs—by drawing on, consuming, arranging, and/or producing a variety of textual materials, including books, periodicals, correspondence, and documents (e.g., manuals, catalogs, lists, recipes, diagrams, charts, and graphs), either in print or online. Typically, adults' participation in literacy practices implies a task to be accomplished or goal to be achieved (e.g., reading a review of a local restaurant, writing a thank-you note, counting money for a purchase). These literacy task demands are ubiquitous in daily life and are often necessary to cope with life demands and function ably in society. Even adults having low-literacy skills engage in a variety of literacy practices—either independently or with the assistance of others, such as family members.

Literacy scholar David Barton (1994) defines *literacy practices* as "the general cultural ways of utilizing written language that people draw upon in their lives . . . what people do with literacy" (p. 44). More specifically, Barton and Hamilton (1998) refer to literacy *events*, which are the specific, observable aspects of literacy practices, for example, using written texts for different purposes, such as a student looking up information about differences between alligators and crocodiles in a book about wildlife for a school science report. Generally, however, surveys of people's literacy practices focus on the broader categories of different kinds of written materials that people use and consume in their daily lives, such as books and newspapers (Smith, 1996). Mellard, Patterson, and Prewett (2007) found that most participants in adult literacy education programs in a Midwestern U.S. state read newspapers and magazines, books, and correspondence regularly. Ninety percent of the participants reported reading newspapers at least occasionally, and nearly as many (87.2%) reported reading books (Mellard et al., 2007). However, these literacy practices varied across different age groups (e.g., older adults read books and work-related materials more frequently than did younger adults).

The literacy practices in which adults engage provide, in a sense, cognitive scaffolds (Reiser, 2004) that can enable the further development of their skills. *Scaffolding* refers to the support that an instructor (or the learning material itself) provides to a learner. According to Sawyer (2006), scaffolds are (or can be) tailored to students' specific learning needs with the intention of helping them achieve their learning goals. So, for example, a functionally illiterate adult might look at picture books and magazines and associate the words on the page with objects depicted in photographs. ABE instructors can reinforce the learners' effort to associate the printed word with the object, decode the word, and pronounce and "read" (comprehend) it. Other kinds of literacy practices, such as listening and speaking with others, can also function as scaffolds for literacy skills development.

ABE participants' literacy practices generally receive less attention from instructors than do learners' literacy skills (i.e., the ability to comprehend or produce written texts). In part, this is likely based on the assumption that, if students' skills are improved, they will be more likely to read and write, do math, and use ICTs. However, the reading materials and tasks employed for skills-based literacy instruction may be highly decontextualized, such as simple texts, or letters, words and phrases in isolation (and, thereby, devoid of context or meaning), or the use of repetitive exercises (e.g., those found in many basal reading workbooks). Adult learners may struggle to find much relevance or "meaning" for such activities and exercises. Some literacy education programs use reading materials that are intended for young children and early readers—basal readers, primers, vocabulary lists, and workbooks—that are not appropriate for adult learners. These kinds of instructional materials are unlike the texts associated with the literacy tasks that adults encounter in their everyday lives. A singular focus on skills development as a consequence of formal instruction, without regard to developing and supporting adult learners' literacy practices, may be shortsighted and ineffective. Sheehan-Holt and Smith (2000), for example, analyzed data from the U.S. National Adult Literacy Survey (NALS) and found that ABE programs had statistically significant effects on learners' literacy practices, but not on their literacy skills.

A limitation of surveys such as the NALS is that the data are cross-sectional and obtained at a single point in time. Thus, it is impossible to determine causal effects of educational program participation on adults' literacy learning and related behaviors. More convincingly, the Portland (Oregon) Longitudinal Study of Adult Learning (LSAL; Reder, 2009) followed a sample of nearly 1,000 adults, ages 18–44, during nearly a decade (1998–2006). About one-half had recently participated or were current participants in adult literacy education and/or basic skills programs in the community. The other half had never participated in any adult literacy or basic skills programs. All of the LSAL participants were school dropouts who had not earned a high school diploma or equivalency and scored below basic literacy proficiency on a standardized reading skills measure.

The study found evidence that participation in basic skills and literacy education programs was unrelated to changes in adults' literacy proficiencies, but was strongly related to changes in their literacy practices. Emphasizing literacy practices is consistent with practice engagement theory (Reder, 1994), which holds that "frequent reading and writing activities lead over a long period of time to greater proficiency" (Reder, 2009, p. 44). Therefore, the takeaway is that it is essential for adult literacy education and basic skills programs to attend to helping adult learners develop a range of practices around literacy.

The available evidence suggests that adult learners may require more than 100 hours of ABE instruction to achieve a single grade-level gain in reading (Sticht, 1989); however, most ABE participants actually complete fewer than 30 hours of instruction (Comings, 2002). Yet, it may be possible to effect positive changes in adult learners' literacy practices in the brief time that they are enrolled in programs through instructor modeling, motivational interventions, or other means.

What is not yet known is how and why participation in ABE contributes to changes in adults' engagement with literacy, in terms of, for example, increasing the frequency and scope of reading books, periodicals, and other text materials at home, within the community, and at work. Several instructional variables, alone or in various combinations, may be responsible for increasing and improving participants' literacy practices. These include instructors' demonstrating, modeling, and/or encouraging specific practices, giving explicit instruction in how (and why) to engage in particular practices, assigning adult learners to read and write different kinds of texts for different purposes, and monitoring and assessing the specific practices in which adult learners participate. Brazilian educator Paulo Freire (1970) advocated that adults learn to read and write so that they can better understand and influence the economic and political conditions of their lives. In his work with rural peasants in South America, he encouraged a critical problem-posing approach in which adult learners draw upon their lives and everyday circumstances as the subjects of study. Rather than using a formally prescribed curriculum, literacy learning is guided by learners' interests, concerns, and social practices (Lewison & Leland, 2002). Freire's work has had significant influence on ABE philosophies and programming over the past four decades. Finally, greater access to and ease of use of ICTs and other digital devices (e.g., smartphones and tablet computers) may also contribute to improving adults' literacy skills and practices, although research with adult basic skills learners is lacking in this area. Therefore, studies are needed to determine the instructional factors that are most important to developing individuals' literacy practices. Simply put, the more that individuals engage in literacy practices, the greater the likelihood they will improve their skills (i.e., comprehension, fluency) over time. ABE programs are encouraged to adopt this principle.

Suggested Cross-References

For more information on concepts and ideas discussed in this article, please see the following articles in the compendium: 7, 12, 13, 14, 18, 19, 21, 23, 24, 31, 35, 54, 57, 61, 69, 70, 71, 78, 80

References

Barton, D. (1994). *Literacy: An introduction to the ecology of written language*. New York, NY: Wiley-Blackwell.

Barton, D., & Hamilton, M. (1998). *Local literacies: Reading and writing in one community*. London, England: Routledge.

Comings, J. (2002). Adult literacy programs. In B. Guzzetti (Ed.), *Literacy in America: An encyclopedia of history, theory, and practice* (pp. 22–25). Santa Barbara, CA: ABC-CLIO.

Freire, P. (1970). *Pedagogy of the oppressed.* New York, NY: Herder & Herder.

Kirsch, I. S., Jungeblut, A., Jenkins, L., & Kolstad, A. (2002). *Adult literacy in America: A first look at the findings of the National Adult Literacy Survey (Vol. 201)*. Washington, DC: National Center for Education, US Department of Education.

Lewison, M., & Leland, C. (2002). Critical literacy. In B. J. Guzzetti (Ed.), *Literacy in America: An encyclopedia of history, theory, and practice* (pp. 108–111). Santa Barbara, CA: ABC-CLIO.

Mellard, D., Patterson, M. B., & Prewett, S. (2007). Literacy practices among adult education participants. *Reading Research Quarterly, 42*(2), 188–213. doi: 10.11598/RR1Q.42.2.1

OECD. (2013). *OECD skills outlook 2013: First results from the survey of adult skills.* Retrieved from http://dx.doi.org/10.1787/9789264204256-en

Reder, S. (1994). Practice engagement theory: A sociocultural approach to literacy across languages and cultures. In R. M. Weber, B. Ferdman, & A. Ramirez (Eds.), *Literacy across languages and cultures* (pp. 33–74). Albany, NY: State University of New York Press.

Reder, S. (2009). Scaling up and moving in: Connecting social practices views to policies and programs in adult education. *Literacy & Numeracy Studies, 16*(2) & *17*(1), 35–50.

Reiser, B. J. (2004). Scaffolding complex learning: The mechanisms of structuring and problematizing student work. *Journal of the Learning Sciences, 13*(3), 273–304.

Sawyer, K. R. (2006). *The Cambridge handbook of the learning sciences*. New York, NY: Cambridge University Press.

Sheehan-Holt, J. K., & Smith, M. C. (2000). Does basic skills education affect adults' literacy proficiencies and reading practices? *Reading Research Quarterly, 35*(2), 226–243.

Smith, M. C. (1996). Differences in reading practices and literacy proficiencies among adults. *Reading Research Quarterly, 31*(2), 196–219.

Sticht, T. G. (1989). Adult literacy education. In E. Z. Rothkopf (Ed.), *Review of research in education* (Vol. 15; pp. 59–96). Washington DC: American Educational Research Association.

Street, B. (1985). *Literacy in theory and practice*. London, England: Cambridge University Press.

What is PIAAC? (n.d.). Retrieved from http://nces.ed.gov/surveys/piaac/

10

GLOBAL CLIMATE CHANGE EDUCATION IS ALL LOCAL

Ankur R. Desai

Keywords: climate change, community organizations, context, elders, engaged, environment, global warming, memory, nature, politically sensitive, social capital, university outreach

Weather is the most watched segment of local television news. Forecasts of the climate for the upcoming season are frequent small talk for most of the general public. But when the topic switches to global warming or climate change, most people clam up, expressing either despondency about our ability to do anything about it or antipathy toward the entire science. Why? There are multiple reasons. Unlike weather or seasonal climate forecasts, the large and complex issue of global warming touches on and potentially threatens the heart of fundamental values of how we live, the role of environmental regulation, and our trust in the communication of scientific knowledge.

So although there is significant demand for knowledge about science, policy, and action of climate change, providing a pathway for a scientist or adult educator to communicate with the public to explain these phenomena is a tricky needle to thread. This article presents a review of practices that have resonated with the public, focusing on elder adult outreach to local organized communities (e.g., church groups, senior centers, community centers) and displays in public settings or newsletters.

Working with older adult communities affords an excellent opportunity to connect changes in a person's lifetime to how scientists detect changes and trends at the global scale. To do so, it is essential to place the global climate trends in context of local weather, regional issues of interest (e.g., farming, fishing, or sea level), and national political environment. A little bit of research on local community issues, whether they relate to agricultural productivity, recreational sport fishing, local causes of flooding, urban heat wave risks, or energy industry jobs, will increase engagement on the topic and acceptance of the speaker as "in the know."

Most national, provincial, or state level agencies have prepared reports and graphics on impacts of climate change regionally. These provide helpful resources for figures with local context. The U.S. National Climate Assessment (Melillo, Richmond, & Yohe, 2014) has excellent chapters on regional impacts and sectorial impacts, with graphics, and a traceability analysis that allows the educator to directly link the finding to the specific research studies from where they were derived. The Wisconsin Initiative on Climate Change Impacts (Katt-Reindeers & Pomplun, 2011) is an example of a state-level approach to climate change impacts on resources important to a particular state.

Recent research has demonstrated that a fact-only approach to controversial political issues actually increases polarization by reinforcing preexisting beliefs based on the level of trust one has with the speaker (Kahan et al., 2012). A "shock-and-awe" approach, with an overwhelming number of figures and graphs, might work for a highly educated, scientifically literate audience, but for many, it is information overload. Focusing first on shared and common concerns at an emotional level and then connecting global challenges to day-to-day realities makes the abstract concept of global warming more relatable. Presenting political options from an open perspective, including conservative and liberal solutions to problems, can enhance discussion and break barriers to trust. An optimistic and empathetic perspective tends to limit negative emotions that can block out understanding (Kiehl, 2016).

Still, one shouldn't shy away from controversial aspects of the topic or dumb down complex scientific phenomena, but rather seek common analogies and concerns and then humanize the science. A speaker needs to have respect for the experience and outlook of the participants, which influences the learning session leader's pace, approachability, and responsiveness. For example, Katherine Hayhoe, a professor at Texas Tech University, tries to connect with her audiences based on her shared Evangelical Christian faith (Hayhoe, 2009). Tom Skilling, chief meteorologist at WGN-TV Chicago, uses his perch and high level of trust locally to connect weather forecasts to a changing climate as part of on-air weather segments. In smaller settings, audience participation activities that involve recalling anecdotal memories of past changes in arrival of flowers or birds, discussing severe weather events, role-playing activities to select among climate change mitigation options, or allowing for anonymous question asking on paper can help better connect an audience on a controversial topic.

Targeting climate outreach to marginalized communities, developing countries, or individual stakeholders of climate-sensitive livelihoods could also be highly worthwhile, as these are the people currently impacted and likely to be hurt by future climate change. The Climate Voices community (Wegner, n.d.), for example, helps connect expert climate scientists to local communities and provides resources to address issues such as facilitating subsistence farming in a changing climate, managing flood risk in low-lying coastal or river valley communities, or confronting social inequality and climate change mitigation. In many cases, older adults have a position of influence in local communities and a goal of older adult outreach would be to ensure that the audience has a set of core key messages to pass onward within and across their respective communities.

A related approach is field-based outdoor activities (e.g., hikes, visits to research sites, or plant identification walks). These can allow for open exchange of local cultural and indigenous knowledge of the land and climate combined with the educator's scientific expertise. In particular, specific expeditions to collect simple observations like local temperature, plant bud burst (e.g., Project Budburst, n.d.), or lake ice thickness might be a perfect segue to place into context a figure showing a long-term trend.

Universities and colleges, especially those with atmospheric or environmental science programs, can help link educators to the public. For example, the University of Wisconsin maintains a database of speakers and helps connect communities to topics. Beyond the sources listed earlier, other excellent online guides include the Environmental Protection Agency's Student's Guide to Climate Change (n.d.) and blogs such as Macroscope by Jon Foley (n.d.).

Climate change outreach and adult education is in high demand. Voters at the ballot box, planners in local communities, and decisions made within individual households all require an understanding of the impacts of climate change and potential options for addressing. Controversy, whether manufactured or real, will always persist. However, direct, measured approaches that connect to audiences can work.

Suggested Cross-References

For more information on concepts and ideas discussed in this article, please see the following articles in the compendium: 1, 5, 6, 11, 19, 35, 47, 52, 56, 57, 59, 65, 66, 67, 70, 80

References

Foley, J. (n.d.). *The macroscope*. Retrieved from https://medium.com/the-macroscope

Hayhoe, K. (n.d.). Katherine Hayhoe: Climate scientist. Retrieved from http://katharinehayhoe.com/wp2016/

Hayhoe, K. (2009). *A climate for change: Global warming facts for faith-based decisions*. Nashville, TN: FaithWords.

Kahan, D., Peters, E., Wittlin, M., Slovic, P., Larrimore-Ouelette, L., Braman, D., & Mandel, G. (2012). The polarizing impact of science literacy and numeracy on perceived climate change risks. *Nature Climate Change, 2*, 732–735. doi: 10.1038/nclimate1547

Katt-Reindeers, E., & Pomplun, S. (Eds.). (2011). *Wisconsin's changing climate: Impacts and adaptation*. Retrieved from http://www.wicci.wisc.edu/report/2011_WICCI-Report.pdf

Kiehl, J. T. (2016). *Facing climate change: An integrated path to the future*. New York, NY: Columbia University Press.

Melillo, J. M., Richmond, T., & Yohe, G. W. (Eds.). (2014). *Climate change impacts in the United States: The third national climate assessment*. U.S. Global Change Research Program, 841 pp. doi: 10.7930/J0Z31WJ2

Project Budburst. (n.d.). Retrieved from http://budburst.org/

U.S. Environmental Protection Agency. (n.d.). *A student's guide to global climate change*. Retrieved from https://www3.epa.gov/climatechange/kids/

Wegner, K. (n.d.). *Climate voices: Science speakers network*. Retrieved from http://climatevoices.org/

SECTION THREE

A BROAD SPECTRUM OF LEARNERS

Articles in this section are about distinctive features of educational program participants and other stakeholders, including educators of adults, each of whom are adult learners who should be understood in relation to their roles, gender, abilities, attitudes, educational level, and diverse life experiences.

11

LIFELONG AND LIFEWIDE LOVING IN EDUCATION

Tamen Jadad-Garcia and Alejandro R. Jadad

Keywords: adults, care, compassion, empower, good, inspire, knowledge, learning, love, meaning, transform, well-being

"Education is an act of love" (Layne & Freire, 1974, p. 34). With this sentence, Paulo Freire, one of the most influential educators of the twentieth century, summarized his pedagogical philosophy and captured the views of a long list of thinkers who, since antiquity and after him, have considered love an essential element of teaching and learning (Yue, 2014).

Countless publications focus on "love of learning" or "love of teaching" (Liston & Garrison, 2004) and on the power of love to transform the entire educational sector (Lin, 2006). More specifically, love has been said to enhance learning (Loreman, 2011), to inspire students and teachers (Fried, 2001), to unite and empower them in the quest for knowledge (Cho, 2005), and to enable them to experience the world with greater sensitivity (Gaita, 2012). None of these authors, from Plato to the most contemporaneous, however, provide an explicit conceptualization of love.

What Is Love?

The meaning of love has remained elusive to artists, scientists, theologians, and philosophers alike (Bergmann, 1987; Berscheid, 2010; Buscaglia, 1996; Fromm, 1956). The typical scenario found in the literature is a text devoted to love in which the authors either avoid explaining its meaning or focus their discussion on one or more types of love, usually of the romantic or erotic kind.

Just as it is the case with other important issues in life, such as health or happiness, it would be unrealistic to find a definition of *love*. A definition, after all, is "an *exact* statement or description of the nature, scope, or meaning of something" (Definition, n.d.). Instead of trying to define *love*, which is likely to be impossible, we have chosen here to try to conceptualize it, by finding words that would likely reflect what we mean when we use it, without requiring an exact description (Blalock, 1982; Coulter, 1973).

A successful conceptualization of love would not only facilitate communication across individuals, disciplines, and sectors but also make the myriad typologies of love less relevant (Berscheid, 2010; Fehr & Russell, 1991) as the same meaning of the word could be applied to different relationships (e.g., self, parental, marital) or intentions (e.g., romantic or erotic).

Here we propose a new conceptualization of love, viewed as the capacity of humans to will good, to do good, to see good, and to feel good.

The Four Components of Love in Education

The role of goodness as the essential virtue of education provides ideal conditions for a conceptualization of love within this context, as it refers to how we treat ourselves, and each other, and how much we live up to our responsibilities (Gardner, 2012). Once we view love through the lens of goodness, very valuable insights start to emerge from theology, philosophy, the arts, and the social sciences.

Willing Good

The first component of this conceptualization of love came from Thomas Aquinas, who characterized love as "to will good" (Crisp, 2014; Gallagher, 1999). Aristotle, who acted as one of the sources of this insight, emphasized that, to will good upon others, to love others, it is essential to love oneself so that our actions are an expression of our internal state (Homiak, 1981). By willing good, first to themselves and then to others, teachers and learners can more easily enjoy the power of their passion, curiosity, and creativity, while becoming more able to achieve happiness and well-being during their educational journey (Liston & Garrison, 2004).

Doing Good

Love has an active component that is clearly expressed by what is considered to be the greatest commandment in most major faiths: "love your neighbor as yourself" (Direct Action and Research Training Center, 2011; Jadad & Davis,

2016). In the New Testament, in particular, every time in which the Hebrew term for love, *ahab*, is used, it could be interpreted as "doing good" (Francis, 2016; Hârlăoanu, 2009; Oord, 2012).

Doing good is also found in the etymological roots of the word for love in other major languages. In Spanish, for instance, the word for love is *amor*. At its core, there is the Indo-European term *amma*, which means mother and mimics the sound that a child would make when calling for help ("Amor," n.d.). The word also contains the Latin suffix *or*, which means "the result of" doing good. Similarly, in English, *love* comes from the Germanic root *Leubh*, which means "to care."

To care and do good for others is crucial in the educational realm. According to Martin (1996), love during learning and teaching is manifested through the conscious and fluid interplay of virtues such as caring, courage, fairness, faithfulness, fidelity, gratitude, honesty, respect, and wisdom.

Sadly, as a result of worries about potential misinterpretation or fear of accusations of impropriety, loving interactions between teachers and students have been "sanitised out of our formal educational contexts" (Loreman, 2011, p. 1). This has contributed to the transformation of formal education into an impersonal and, as a result, a less effective endeavor (Sarason, 2002; Wise, 2008). By bringing back the power and beauty of willing and doing good, ethical concerns might be more easily overcome through a more successful discussion. Also, actions in the spirit of love can occur within the context of learning and teaching, which can open new opportunities for strong bonds between teachers and students to emerge (Liston & Garrison, 2004).

Seeing Good

This element of perception is very much rooted in loving and is emphasized by various philosophies including Sufism, which closely associates love with "seeing good" no matter the circumstances (Ramakrishnan, 2010), which echoes the views of the Stoics, particularly Epictetus and Marcus Aurelius (Hadot, 1998). Along these same lines, Nietzsche brought us the term *amor fati*, to reflect the importance of perceiving as positive even the most horrible events (Stern, 2013).

This capacity to see good could be very valuable in education, as it would enable teachers and learners alike to face negative events in a constructive way, resisting frustration and developing high levels of resilience in and out of the classroom (Duckworth, Peterson, Matthews, & Kelly, 2007).

Feeling Good

Lastly, Freire himself offered another element to complete the conceptualization of love, "to feel good," particularly when it happens in the company of others (Rossatto, 2008). For most teachers, this is the main driving force for their vocation (Liston & Garrison, 2004), as the ability to touch other people's lives deeply acts as a strong motivator and reinforcement of their behavior. Doing good also feels good (Anik, Aknin, Norton, & Dunn, 2009) and triggers reciprocity among the learners, and vice versa, acts of kindness by students motivate goodness among the teachers (Clegg & Rowland, 2010). These positive feelings also have the capacity to enhance cognitive and behavioral abilities and support the maintenance of mental health, while enhancing learning, strengthening bonds, improving communication, and providing a sense of comfort and security to all involved (Garland et al., 2010).

Toward Lifelong and Lifewide Loving

In the years that followed World War II, adult education was inspired by its perceived potential contributions to human flourishing. During UNESCO's founding conference in London in 1945, the American delegation presented a resolution urging the organization's involvement in adult education because "it has an immediate contribution to make to the enlightenment of the citizens of the world" (United Nations, 1945, p. 73). Four years later, when UNESCO held the First International Conference on Adult Education, its director-general stressed, "to educate is to liberate" (Hely, 1962, p. 31). From that point on, lifelong learning, which has a history dating back at least to the Renaissance, was brought progressively to the forefront of adult education to encompass its nonformal modalities. It was hoped that it would provide viable answers to the global challenges of the twentieth century and beyond, including the promotion of peace and human rights, respect for diversity and conflict resolution, economic and ecological sustainability, and transformation of work. A complementary approach that had been developing since the 1920s, known as lifewide learning, was proposed as an additional means to boost the transformative effects of education by enabling learning in all contexts and spaces of daily life (Jackson, 2012).

Throughout the remaining years of the twentieth century, however, the scope of lifelong learning narrowed under the weight of massive economic and political interests, which turned it into a process focused on "giving people skills" to find work, while they are trapped in an endless vicious cycle of "training and the acquisition of skills to make a living" (Elfert, 2016, p. 75). Lifewide learning never received the enthusiastic support from the educational or political establishment that was expected, remaining little more than a fringe proposition.

Now that we live in an interconnected world full of challenges that threaten our survival as a species with rapid deterioration of the environment; widening social and economic gaps; political and ideological polarization; and pandemic levels of work-related stress, anxiety, and depression, we must recover the humanist spirit that led to the creation of UNESCO, the rebirth of the lifelong learning movement, and the proposal for lifewide learning. Love might be the vital force that could make it happen.

Thanks to the fast pace with which robots and computer-driven algorithms are promising to liberate humans from repetitive, mindless tasks and progressively strong calls for the introduction of a minimum income that would secure the basic needs of all people (Ford, 2015), we could be at the threshold of a new era, one in which love could enrich learning, throughout all stages of life, from cradle to grave, and within all aspects and spaces of daily living.

Imbuing lifelong and lifewide learning with love does not require institutional support, costly infrastructures, or sophisticated curricular development processes. All that is needed for love to permeate education is awareness of its importance, and recognition that willing, doing, seeing, and feeling good are essential components of truly transformative teaching and learning experiences. Love could also help unleash, once and for all, the liberating power of education. Augustine of Hippo knew the capacity of love to set us free when he opened his "love sermon" with the Latin dictum *Ama, et fac quod vis*, which means, *"Love and do what you will"* (TeSelle, 2006, p. 50). He then continued with a message that would easily resonate among teachers and learners across locations and ages:

> *If you hold your peace, hold your peace out of love.*
> *If you cry out, cry out in love.*
> *If you correct someone, correct them out of love.*
> *If you spare them, spare them out of love.*
> *Let the root of love be in you: nothing can spring from it but good.* (p. 50)

The time has come for adult education to harness the power of love. By doing so, it could live up to the aspirational hopes of those who viewed it as a human right, as a source of freedom, as a means to achieving a full life, and as a viable way to create a radically different society in which we could all enjoy long, healthy, happy lives as passengers of a flourishing planet.

Suggested Cross-References

For more information on concepts and ideas discussed in this article, please see the following articles in the compendium: 1, 2, 5, 6, 7, 10, 12, 14, 19, 22, 35, 52, 54, 57, 58, 59, 66, 69, 70, 71, 79, 80

References

Amor. (n.d.). In *Diccionario Etimológico.* Retrieved from http://etimologias.dechile.net/?amor

Anik, L., Aknin, L. B., Norton, M. I., & Dunn, E. W. (2009). *Feeling good about giving: The benefits (and costs) of self-interested charitable behavior* (Harvard Business School Marketing Unit Working Paper No. 10-012). Retrieved from http://ssrn.com/abstract=1444831

Bergmann, M. S. (1987). *The anatomy of loving: The story of man's quest to know what love is*. New York, NY: Columbia University Press.

Berscheid, E. (2010). Love in the fourth dimension. *Annual Review of Psychology, 61*, 1–25.

Blalock, H. M. (1982). *Conceptualization and measurement in the social sciences*. Beverly Hills, CA: Sage Publications Inc.

Buscaglia, L. F. (1996). *Love: What life is all about.* New York, NY: Ballantine Books.

Cho, D. (2005). Lessons of love: Psychoanalysis and teacher–student love. *Educational Theory, 55*(1), 79–96.

Clegg, S., & Rowland, S. (2010). Kindness in pedagogical practice and academic life. *British Journal of Sociology of Education, 31*(6), 719–735.

Coulter, J. (1973). Language and the conceptualization of meaning. *Sociology, 7*(2), 173–189.

Crisp, R. (Ed.). (2014). *Aristotle: Nicomachean ethics.* Cambridge, UK: Cambridge University Press.

Direct Action and Research Training Center. (2011, June 11). To love your neighbor as yourself: An interfaith perspective on the great commandment. [Blog]. Retrieved from http://thedartcenter.org/call-to-justice/2011/06/to-love-your-neighbor-as-yourself-an- interfaith-perspective-on-the-great-commandment/_

Definition. (n.d.). In *Oxford dictionaries*. Retrieved from https://en.oxforddictionaries.com/definition/definition

Duckworth, A. L., Peterson, C., Matthews, M. D., & Kelly, D. R. (2007). Grit: Perseverance and passion for long-term goals. *Journal of Personality and Social Psychology, 92*(6), 1087.

Elfert, M. (2016). *The utopia of lifelong learning: An intellectual history of UNESCO's humanistic approach to education, 1945–2015* (Doctoral dissertation). University of British Columbia, Canada.

Fehr, B., & Russell, J. A. (1991). The concept of love viewed from a prototype perspective. *Journal of Personality and Social Psychology, 60*(3), 425–438.

Ford, M. (2015). *Rise of the robots: Technology and the threat of a jobless future.* New York, NY: Basic Books.

Francis. (2016). *Amoris Laetitia.* Retrieved from https://w2.vatican.va/content/dam/francesco/pdf/apost_exhortations/documents/papa-francesco_esortazione-ap_20160319_amoris-laetitia_en.pdf

Fried, R. L. (2001). *The passionate teacher: A practical guide.* Boston, MA: Beacon Press.

Fromm, E. (1956). *The art of loving.* London, England: Thorsons.

Gaita, R. (2012). Love and teaching: Renewing a common world. *Oxford Review of Education, 38*(6), 761–769.

Gallagher, D. M. (1999). Thomas Aquinas on self-love as the basis for love of others. *Acta Philosophica, 8*(1), 23–44.

Gardner, H. (2012). *Truth, beauty, and goodness reframed: Educating for the virtues in the age of truthiness and twitter*. New York, NY: Basic Books.

Garland, E. L., Fredrickson, B., Kring, A. M., Johnson, D. P., Meyer, P. S., & Penn, D. L. (2010). Upward spirals of positive emotions counter downward spirals of negativity: Insights from the broaden-and-build theory and affective neuroscience on the treatment of emotion dysfunctions and deficits in psychopathology. *Clinical Psychology Review, 30*(7), 849–864.

Hadot, P. (1998). *The inner citadel: The meditations of Marcus Aurelius*. Cambridge, MA: Harvard University Press.

Hârlăoanu, C. P. (2009). The main Hebrew words for love: Ahab and Hesed. *Analele Ştiinţifice ale Universităţii "Alexandru Ioan Cuza"din Iaşi. Teologie Ortodoxă, 1*, 51–66.

Hely, A. S. (1962). *New trends in adult education: From Elsinore to Montreal*. Paris, France: UNESCO.

Homiak, M. L. (1981). Virtue and self-love in Aristotle's ethics. *Canadian Journal of Philosophy, 11*(4), 633–651.

Jackson, N. J. (2012). Lifewide learning: History of an idea. *The Lifewide Learning, Education & Personal Development e-book*, 1–30.

Jadad, A. R., & Davis, D. (2016). What do we need to protect, at all costs, during the 21st century? Reflections from a curated, interactive co-created intellectual jazz performance. *Journal of Continuing Education in the Health Professions, 36*, S27–S31.

Layne, A., & Freire, P. (1974). Education for critical consciousness. *The Journal of Educational Thought, 8*(3), 159–161.

Lin, J. (2006). *Love, peace, and wisdom in education: A vision for education in the 21st century*. Lanham, MD: Rowman & Littlefield Education.

Liston, D. P., & Garrison, J. W. (Eds.). (2004). *Teaching, learning, and loving: Reclaiming passion in educational practice*. New York, NY: Routledge.

Loreman, T. (2011). *Love as pedagogy*. Rotterdam, The Netherlands: Sense.

Martin, M. W. (1996). *Love's virtues*. Lawrence, KS: University Press of Kansas.

Oord, T. J. (2012). Love, Wesleyan theology, and psychological dimensions of both. *Journal of Psychology and Christianity, 31*(2), 144–157.

Ramakrishnan, R. (2010). *Many paths, one destination: Love, peace, compassion, tolerance, and understanding through world religions*. Tucson, AZ: Wheatmark.

Rossatto, C. A. (2008). Freire's understanding of history, current reality, and future aspirations. *Journal of Thought, 43*(1&2), 149–161.

Sarason, S. B. (2002). *Educational reform: A self-scrutinizing memoir*. New York, NY: Teachers College Press.

Stern, T. (2013, July). VIII—Nietzsche, Amor Fati and the Gay Science. In *Proceedings of the Aristotelian Society* (Vol. 113, No. 2 Part 2, pp. 145–162).

TeSelle, E. (2006). *Augustine the theologian*. Eugene, OR: Abingdon Press.

United Nations. (1945). *Conference for the establishment of the United Nations Educational, Scientific and Cultural Organization.* Retrieved from http://unesdoc.unesco.org/images/0011/001176/117626e.pdf

Wise, B. (2008). High schools at the tipping point. *Educational Leadership, 65*(8), 8–13.

Yue, F. (2014). *Teaching as an act of love* (Doctoral dissertation). Auckland University of Technology, Auckland, New Zealand.

12

ADULT LEARNERS WITH DISABILITIES

Overcoming Invisibility and Exclusion

Carol Rogers-Shaw

Keywords: access, action research, agencies, collective, difference, disability, distance, educational and economic opportunity, emancipatory research, impairment, improvements, inclusion, individual, obstacles, participation, policy, social justice, social model, socioeconomic, values

The field of adult education needs to address disability and the increasing presence of people with disabilities (PWD) in adult education. In 2006, the Convention on the Rights of Persons with Disabilities (CRPD) acknowledged that "the 650 million people in the world living with disabilities . . . lack the opportunities of the mainstream population. They encounter a myriad of physical and social obstacles" (United Nations, 2007, para. 2); however, more than a decade later, there is still limited focus on disability in adult education. Understanding the historical context of disability and its connection to social justice is vital to educators, program administrators, policymakers, and researchers involved in educating adults in a variety of contexts so adult learners can be better served.

The United Nations (2006) defines *disability* as "an evolving concept and that disability results from the interaction between persons with impairments and attitudinal and environmental barriers that hinder their full and effective participation in society on an equal basis with others" (p. 1). The definition of *disability* has changed over time, affected by historical context and societal shifts. The view of disability as a predominantly medical problem or unfortunate personal tragedy was common until after World War II when there was an increase in veterans with disabilities, a greater number of elderly citizens with disabilities due to advances in medicine, and a heightened role of social movements in supporting the rights of PWD. At that time, governments and social agencies became more involved in providing services to PWD (Barnes, 2012).

The social model developed from the work of the Union of the Physically Impaired Against Segregation (UPIAS) in Britain in the 1970s. UPIAS described disability as social exclusion caused by public structures and systems as opposed to impairment due to the individual's specific limitation. This distinction is significant for adult education that both opposes societal restrictions and teaches the individual. Shakespeare and Watson (2002) discussed the complexity of disability and the need to look beyond the social model, and Barnes (2003) credited the work of UPIAS with politicizing disability and establishing emancipatory disability research similar to critical social research and participatory action research on issues of race, gender, and sexual orientation. Barnes (2003) noted that much of disability research has focused on "impairment, whether physical, sensory or intellectual, [as] the primary cause of 'disability' and therefore [also] the difficulties: economic, political and cultural, encountered by people labelled 'disabled'" (p. 4). *Implementing the Social Model of Disability: Theory and Research* edited by Colin Barnes and Geof Mercer (2004) contains valuable chapters on theory and research related to the social model.

A major development of CRPD was the shift from viewing disability as an issue for nations to address through social welfare programs to acknowledging that disability is a human rights concern. Article 24 of the treaty establishes the rights of PWD to "adult education and lifelong learning without discrimination and on an equal basis with others" (United Nations, 2006, p. 18). Despite a clear call for inclusion of PWD, factors that negatively affect implementation include the level of understanding of disability within society, the presence of stereotypical views of disability, the lack of focus on the capabilities of PWD, and the history of disability legislation and education within individual nations. Adult education faces issues that are significant to learners with disabilities, including the distribution of power, the ability to gain access, and the need for inclusion that establishes equity.

Adult education focuses on seeing difference, recognizing its importance, and finding positives in interdependence where "one strives for individual needs alongside communitarian needs, where the community values, celebrates and responds energetically to diversity" (Goodley, 2011, p. 151); this is the description of inclusive education. Increasingly, literacy and numeracy instruction, vocational education courses, programs for veterans, immigrant education, distance education opportunities, and higher education environments all serve learners with disabilities.

Patterson (2008) reviewed the weak literacy skills of PWD, the correlation between learning disability in adults and low socioeconomic status, and adult literacy programs. Gregg (2007) noted the lack of success in schooling that results in fewer job opportunities, less opportunity for advancement, and lower socioeconomic status for PWD leading to a need for vocational training; he also discussed higher education's failure to adequately address those needs. If a goal of adult education is to create a more equitable society by supporting marginalized groups, providing access to postsecondary education that improves employability is important. Sandmann (2010) argued that earning a higher education degree can provide PWD with enhanced employment opportunities, increased standard of living, more significant participation in civil society, and greater social mobility. Madaus, Miller, and Vance (2009) focused on veterans with both visible physical disabilities and invisible disabilities such as post-traumatic stress disorder (PTSD) and depression. The rise in the number of individuals with learning disabilities and mental illnesses in postsecondary education (Hunt & Eisenberg, 2010; Madaus & Shaw, 2010) highlights invisible disabilities that need attention. Learning disabilities can also complicate immigrants' ability to become fluent in a new language. Lyman and Figgins (2005) explored power relationships and exclusion based on a lack of fluency. The impairments of online learners may be invisible in distance education, but these students have increasingly turned to online courses because they offer unique opportunities. Bozkurt and colleagues (2015) noted the shift in views of distance learning toward general acceptance and mainstream participation so those with disabilities are now more likely to experience distance education.

There is a need for inclusion of PWD in adult education in order to meet the goal of equity. Goodley (2011) states, "[d]isability and social justice meet at the crossroads of inclusive education" (p. 138). Adult education needs to embrace the position of the disability movement that demands that PWD be included whether by resisting disabling social structures or by improving learning for individuals with impairments.

Suggested Cross-References

For more information on concepts and ideas discussed in this article, please see the following articles in the compendium: 1, 2, 5, 6, 7, 8, 9, 11, 13, 14, 18, 19, 25, 33, 35, 37, 42, 52, 54, 56, 57, 61, 70, 71, 80

References

Barnes, C. (2003). What a difference a decade makes: Reflections on doing "emancipatory" disability research. *Disability & Society, 18*(1), 3–17.

Barnes, C. (2012). Understanding the social model of disability: Past, present and future. In N. Watson, A. Roulstone, & C. Thomas (Eds.), *Routledge handbook of disability studies* (pp. 12–29). London, England: Routledge.

Barnes, C., & Mercer, G. (Eds.). (2004). *Implementing the social model of disability: Theory and research.* Leeds, UK: Disability Press.

Bozkurt, A., Akgun-Ozbek, E., Yilmazel, S., Erdogdu, E., Ucar, H., Guler, E., . . . Hakan Aydin, C. (2015). Trends in distance education research: A content analysis of journals 2009–2013. *International Review of Research in Open and Distributed Learning American Journal of Distance Education (AJDE), 16*(1), 330–363.

Goodley, D. (2011). *Disability studies: An interdisciplinary introduction.* Los Angeles, CA: SAGE.

Gregg, N. (2007). Underserved and unprepared: Postsecondary learning disabilities. *Learning Disabilities Research & Practice, 22*(4), 219–228.

Hunt, J., & Eisenberg, D. (2010). Mental health problems and help-seeking behavior among college students. *Journal of Adolescent Health, 46*(1), 3–10.

Lyman, H., & Figgins, M. (2005). Democracy, dialect, and the power of every voice. *English Journal, 94*(5), 40–47.

Madaus, J., Miller, W., & Vance, M. (2009). Veterans with disabilities in postsecondary education. *Journal of Postsecondary Education and Disability, 22*(1), 10–17.

Madaus, J., & Shaw, S. (2010). College as a realistic option for students with learning disabilities. *InfoSheets.* Overland Park, KS: Council for Learning Disabilities.

Patterson, M. (2008). Learning disability prevalence and adult education program characteristics. *Learning Disabilities Research & Practice, 23*(1), 50–59.

Sandmann, L. (2010). Adults in four-year colleges and universities: Moving from the margins to the mainstream? In C. Kasworm, A. Rose, & J. Ross-Gordon (Eds.), *Handbook of adult and continuing education* (9th ed.; pp. 221–230). Los Angeles, CA: SAGE.

Shakespeare, T., & Watson, N. (2002). The social model of disability: An outdated ideology? *Research in Social Science and Disability, 2*, 9–28.

United Nations. (2006). *Convention on the rights of persons with disabilities.* Retrieved from http://www.un.org/disabilities/documents/convention/convoptprot-e.pdf

United Nations. (2007). *Frequently asked questions regarding the convention on the rights of persons with disabilities.* Retrieved from http://www.un.org/esa/socdev/enable/convinfofaq.htm#top

13

ADULTS WITH LOW LITERACY SKILLS

Theoretical Perspectives Toward Understanding Teaching and Learning

Maurice C. Taylor, David L. Trumpower, and Edward R. Purse

Keywords: access, adult learners, attitudes, construction, contexts, formal and informal learning, knowledge, literacy, marginal, motivation, participation, policy, practitioners, prepared, proficiency, progress, self-direction, social capital, social learning theories, sociocultural, success

This article focuses on an important learner—the adult with low literacy skills. Across the global enterprise of adult education, practitioners need to become more aware of the characteristics of this marginalized group of adults. Therefore, the intention of this article is to highlight the profile of this learner through the lens of different sociocultural theories to help guide decisions for effective teaching into the future. Learning contexts and adults with low literacy skills are two main themes in the scholarly literature. Drawing from Organization for Economic Co-operation and Development (OECD) and other country reports, Werquin (2010) suggests that the definition of *learning context* is subject to debate. However, formal education and informal learning may be considered the two extremities of a learning continuum, with nonformal learning situated somewhere in between, depending on national and local perspectives. In this overview, three learning contexts provide the backdrop to profile adult learners with low literacy skills, each through a theoretical lens that helps explain the teaching and learning process. The first profile—the adult basic education (ABE) learner in the formal setting—is viewed through a motivational framework for culturally responsive teaching and a social capital theory. The adult with low literacy as a lifelong learner engaging in informal learning is the second profile and is explored through social constructivism. The third relates to essential skills training of the adult worker as seen through social cognitive theory (Essential Skills Ontario, 2012).

The theoretical perspectives draw largely from observations made from our involvement in two projects. The first was a 4-year mixed methods study of workers engaged in lifelong learning through workplace skills training programs across Manitoba and Nova Scotia, and adult learners in an ABE high school program in Ontario, Canada. The second was a 3-year participatory action research design where the essential skills needs of adult workers and students at 9 workplace sites and 17 community colleges across Canada were assessed, and interventions developed and implemented (Taylor, Trumpower, & Pavic, 2013; Taylor & Trumpower, 2014; Taylor, Trumpower, & Purse, 2015).

The ABE Learner in Formal Education

In this first profile we examine the motivation and preparedness of ABE learners engaged in formal classroom education and how teachers might help foster both factors. In Wlodkowski's motivational framework for culturally responsive teaching (2011), four key conditions—establishing inclusion, developing positive attitudes, enhancing meaning, and engendering competence—provide the basis around which teachers can develop pedagogical strategies to create intrinsically motivating conditions for diverse learners. Taylor and Trumpower (2014) showed how ABE teachers can enact such motivating conditions by establishing a respectful atmosphere where students feel connected to each other as well as the instructor; make connections between the classroom experience and the workplace; identify student interests, goals, and backgrounds; and provide encouragement and opportunities for engaging in self-directed and collaborative activities. We further expanded Wlodkowski's framework by highlighting how *extrinsic* factors, such as realistic job entry goals and social capital, can influence learning.

Kilpatrick, Field, and Falk (2003) describe social capital as a resource based on relationships among people, including friendships, workplace ties, and involvement in professional communities of practice. These authors specify that social capital is built from two types of resources: (a) the knowledge of who, when, and where to go for support toward accomplishing some goal; and (b) identification of resources and the ability to provide support of oneself through self-confidence, reciprocity, and shared values. As noted by Taylor and colleagues (2013), ABE learners may develop social capital within formal learning settings through the support of literacy teachers who establish these motivational conditions, or they may become more aware of existing social capital through activities such as collaboration, self-directed learning, and knowledge sharing in a classroom.

The Adult With Low Literacy as a Lifelong Learner

The second profile involves engaging adults with low literacy as lifelong learners in informal learning through social constructivism. As Edwards (2009) asks, "If learning is lifelong and life wide, then what specifically is the learning context?" (p. 1). To the social constructivist, learning is a social process shaped by social activity. Interactions with anyone or any social object may therefore create an informal learning context. Although informal learning in social contexts is often viewed as naturally occurring, Merrifield (2012) points to the influence of context and culture in learning. Kling (2012) also suggests that learning is highly influenced by learners' perceptions of who they are and how they believe the world views them. For adults with low literacy skills, informal learning may be a challenge as their perceptions of themselves and their ability to meaningfully engage in social interactions may limit their participation. In addition, learning potential is also influenced by an adult's motivation. As Kling (2012) further states, learner self-perception is improved by acknowledged success. This highlights recent efforts to recognize informal learning and, as Werquin (2010) notes, such learning is high on the national policy agendas of many OECD countries. However, Taylor and colleagues (2015) suggest that this is not the case in Canada, particularly for adults with low skills. Nevertheless, the degree to which other countries have succeeded continues to be of value. For lifelong learners, the degree to which adults with low literacy believe they can learn and the motivation to do so may be significantly influenced by social context.

The Adult Worker in Essential Skills Training

Workers acquiring essential skills are the focus of this third profile. In a recent study that investigated the learning trajectories of Canadian workers enrolled in essential skills training, it was found that the critical factors that influenced their learning processes could be understood through the lens of social cognitive theory (Taylor et al., 2015). Importantly, this sociocultural approach moves beyond the immediate learning context and encapsulates both the internal and external factors of the educational process through a concept called *reciprocal determinism*. This concept brings the interaction of environmental events, personal factors, and behaviors together in the process of learning (Bussey & Bandura, 1999). Many countries have already developed government-sponsored work-related training initiatives by focusing on partnership development and building teams to support training initiatives and learning centers. Taken together, such elements can be viewed as environmental events—a cornerstone of reciprocal determinism.

Additionally, the results of worker needs assessments, increases in job satisfaction, attitudes toward learning, and voluntary participation in essential skills training can also be considered personal factors. These constitute another concept embedded in social cognitive theory. Finally, elements such as persistence and effort by the worker in the training program as well as self-regulation of progress based on assessment feedback can be viewed as behaviors. As Schunk (2004) suggests, the interplay of the physical learning environment coupled with worker beliefs, actions, and goals provide a way of understanding the context, content, and characteristics of the adult worker acquiring essential literacy skills.

Implications

For the adult education practitioner, becoming aware of the underlying motivation for each of these three types of learners is critical. Coming to know the driving force for learner participation can act as the catalyst for determining content and instructional techniques and the meaning of progress. Professional development and training for practitioners regarding how these motivational factors can be integrated within curriculum and evaluation can enhance positive learner autonomy. Turning to the adult education researcher, questions still remain as to how sociocultural conditions can influence learners' perceptions of self and growth in their various life roles. Such questions can be investigated in research designs that foster partnerships with adult learners, such as participatory action research. Furthermore, there is a real need for practitioners to disseminate findings of this nature at conferences and venues alongside academics. At a policy level, much can also be learned from the *Eurydice Report* (European Commission, 2015), especially if the literacy field is to widen access of learning opportunities for adult learners in any of the contexts profiled here. Related to this policy concern is the importance of ensuring that formal, nonformal, and informal learning is recognized by educational institutions and employers. Creating a momentum for this requires that national associations and agencies in adult education work in concert to place this issue on international agendas.

Suggested Cross-References

For more information on concepts and ideas discussed in this article, please see the following articles in the compendium: 4, 9, 12, 14, 19, 21, 23, 25, 31, 35, 37, 51, 52, 53, 61, 70, 71, 76, 77, 78, 79, 80

References

Bussey, K., & Bandura, A. (1999). Social cognitive theory of gender development and differentiation. *Psychological Review, 106*(4), 676–713.

Edwards, R. (2009). Introduction: Life as a learning context? In R. Edwards, G. Biesta, M. Thorpe (Eds.), *Rethinking contexts for learning and teaching: Communities, activities and networks* (pp. 1–13). Abingdon, Oxon, UK: Routledge.

Essential Skills Ontario. (2012). *Menial no more: A discussion paper advancing our workforce through digital skills*. Toronto, Ontario: Author.

European Commission. (2015). *Adult education and training in Europe: Widening access to learning opportunities. Eurydice Report*. Luxembourg, Publications Office of the European Union.

Kilpatrick, S., Field, J., & Falk, I. (2003). Social capital: An analytical tool for exploring lifelong learning and community development. *British Educational Research Journal, 29*(3), 417–433.

Kling, M. (2012). Examining the links between self-perception and adult learning: Highlighting the parallels for educators and learners. *The International Institute of Social and Economic Sciences International Interdisciplinary Conference Proceedings*, Palermo, Sicily.

Merrifield, J. (2012). *Ecologies of learning: How culture and context impact outcomes of workplace literacy and essential skills*. Quebec, Canada: Centre for Literacy of Quebec.

Schunk, D. (2004). *Learning theories: An educational perspective* (4th ed.). Columbus, OH: Merrill/Prentice-Hall.

Taylor, M., & Trumpower, D. (2014). Adult high school learners: Engaging conditions in the teaching and learning process. *International Forum of Teaching and Studies, 10*(2), 3–12.

Taylor, M., Trumpower, D., & Pavic, I. (2013). Unravelling the lifelong learning process for Canadian workers and adult learners acquiring higher skills. *Journal of Research and Practice for Adult Literacy, Secondary, and Basic Education, 2*(2), 101–113.

Taylor, M., Trumpower, D., & Purse, E. (2015). The role of work-related learning in the identity transformation of Canadian workers with low literacy skills. *International Review of Education, 61(1)*, 815–833.

Werquin, P. (2010). *Recognizing non-formal and informal learning: Outcomes, policies and practices.* Paris, France: OECD Publishing.

Wlodkowski, R. J. (2011). *Enhancing adult motivation to learn: A comprehensive guide for teaching all adults*. Hoboken, NJ: John Wiley & Sons.

14

THE POWER TO CHANGE LIVES

The University of Wisconsin–Madison Odyssey Project

Emily Auerbach

Keywords: accessible, arts, caring, change, community, diverse, family members, humanities, land-grant learners, library, literacy, low income, nontraditional, opportunity, outreach, provider, self, subsidy, teach, transformation

An African American man starting over after incarceration and homelessness writes, "The Odyssey Project helped me unwrap my gifts and rewrite the story of my life." "Transformative education" and "lifelong learning" are not just slogans or catchphrases for us; they capture a reality happening each Wednesday night in a low-income neighborhood in Madison, Wisconsin, as we offer free of charge a 2-semester, 6-credit humanities course designed to empower adults at the poverty level to overcome adversity and achieve dreams through higher education. Our hard-won successes over the past 14 years of the program may offer insights to others around the world seeking to raise retention rates for low-income, first-generation college students from racially diverse backgrounds who view themselves as "not college material."

Editor's note: Many educators of adults seek greater diversity in their programs. This article about an award-winning program at the University of Wisconsin–Madison (UW–Madison) illustrates an effective option for engaging underrepresented minorities in a jumpstart college humanities course. As you read Emily Auerbach's personal narrative of launching and directing the Odyssey Project for over a decade, consider implications for your own local programs and interests.

Prior to starting the University of Wisconsin (UW) Odyssey Project, I had already spent two decades as an English professor at UW–Madison charged with an outreach mission, conducting programs on literature for nontraditional adult students in retirement centers, prisons, Elderhostels, public libraries, service clubs, the backs of grocery stores, over the radio, and online. More than in the traditional campus classes I taught, I found that nontraditional students craved instruction that lifted the material off the page and into their own lives.

Knowing of my outreach work, Jean Feraca (a colleague of mine at Wisconsin Public Radio) approached me about starting a new program. She had been inspired by a guest on her talk show, Earl Shorris, an award-winning author and revolutionary educational reformer known for having started the Clemente Course in the Humanities (www.clementecourse.org). Jean was thoroughly intrigued by his account of teaching philosophy, literature, history, and art history to the poor in ways that could bring about a transformation and begin a journey out of poverty. How might we start a Clemente Course in the Humanities in Madison?

What Jean did not know was that my own family's story of escape from poverty through a free liberal arts education would shape my approach to the undertaking. I wanted not just a "great works" class but a four-year, free college education for those wanting to break a cycle of generational poverty. My mother had come from Appalachia, born into an impoverished region 12 miles from Knoxville, Tennessee, with no running water. Teachers who saw she was an avid reader told her about a chance for the poor to receive higher education in neighboring Kentucky at progressive Berea College. She arrived on campus with a wardrobe consisting of one skirt and two blouses, with no extra spending money. Had someone said "you must buy an expensive textbook," she would have had to go home. Berea changed her life. After graduating valedictorian, she continued on to advanced degrees from Columbia University and UW–Madison.

While at Berea, she met my father, there as an "other" allowed in for diversity at a Christian school. My father's story of poverty was that of the immigrant. Fleeing Nazi Germany, my father's parents lost everything, including the ability to practice their careers as lawyers. Berea offered a chance to get a liberal arts education to those whose families had little or no money. After Berea, my father went on to become an internationally recognized scientist, and in 2017 he received Berea's distinguished alumnus award (Berea College, 2015).

When I speak of the UW Odyssey Project, I mention my parents' story because it cuts through stereotypes that I otherwise encounter when speaking about "the poor" or "low-income students" from "diverse backgrounds."

Administrators cautioning me about starting a program here in Madison remarked, "Poor people aren't going to want to study Plato, and you'll have trouble filling a class." Clemente course directors warned, "You'll be lucky if you end up with half the at-risk students you start with." Although I loved Earl Shorris's (2010) revolutionary concept of providing the best works of moral philosophy, literature, history, and art free of charge to those trapped in poverty, I cringed at the title of his book: *Riches for the Poor*. My mother *had* riches inside her when she arrived at Berea College; she just lacked the opportunity (as my Odyssey student later put it) "to unwrap [her] gifts." Also, I would argue that the 400 "poor" students I have encountered in the 14 years of working on the UW Odyssey Project have enriched others through their voices and visions. The concept of "riches for the poor" makes me picture well-meaning colonialists arriving with boxes of Plato and Shakespeare for the benighted poor, and that somehow did not square with my growing recognition of the eloquence and insight of the diverse adults I was working with each week. In an effort to make our program more reciprocal, to engage adult students more directly in the material, we add in the arts—creative writing, journalism, music—and encourage our students to respond in original ways to the material we read.

We decided not to run our program as an official Clemente course through New York's Bard College but instead to build it directly into UW–Madison. Being a "Clemente-inspired" course gave us the freedom to vary the curriculum, to add in the arts, and to grant our students six credits from UW, one of the top universities in the world. Since its early days, UW prided itself on something called "the Wisconsin Idea" (www.wisc.edu/wisconsin-idea) As UW's former president Charles Van Hise articulated back in 1905, the boundaries of the university should be the boundaries of the state. Why not find ways to make the treasures of this land-grant institution available to the citizens whose taxes helped support its existence?

The UW Odyssey Project epitomizes the Wisconsin Idea in action. On a typical Wednesday night, an unlikely group of 30 low-income adults of color admitted as "special students" to UW–Madison discusses Walt Whitman's "Song of Myself"; Plato's account of Socrates's trial and death; the Declaration of Independence; the meaning of *onomatopoeia* and *agoraphobia*; the logical arguments in Martin Luther King Jr.'s "Letter from Birmingham Jail"; or the difference between Doric, Ionic, and Corinthian columns in ancient architecture. Yes, they are earning college credits and gaining practical skills in writing, reading comprehension, and critical thinking. But the experience affects them at a much deeper level as well, as they are encouraged to make and remake the material, to transform it into something with direct meaning in their lives. Plato's "Allegory of the Cave" reminds one student of the trap of drug addiction and another of domestic abuse. One student recasts a scene from *Macbeth* (Shakespeare & Muir, 2013) in Chicago with Lady Macbeth urging her husband to "be a man" and shoot Duncan while he has a chance. In the hands of a student who has faced homelessness, Dickens's Ebenezer Scrooge becomes a heartless Madison landlord.

Those of us who teach the humanities often feel on the defensive, as if justifying the value of material deemed impractical or fanciful. Reading Emily Dickinson does not pay the rent. Acting out scenes from Shakespeare puts no food in the refrigerator. So how does one justify teaching the humanities to adults battling poverty?

I would argue that in addition to promoting literacy, a key pathway to transformation, exposure to the humanities changes one's sense of self in profoundly important ways. After reading poems by Whitman, Dickinson, Langston Hughes, and others, we ask our students to write their own poems and creative essays, including creating metaphors about themselves and their lives. "My life is a revolving door," writes one student, "because just when I think I'm starting to get somewhere, my drug-using friends drag me back around to the other side and I'm stuck again." To envision her life that way marks the first step to change. Pride in self emerges as students find their voices and discover their stories have power. Our student newsletter ("Odyssey Oracle") provides a chance to showcase students' writings; some students go on to publish their editorials and stories in other places, read them on the radio or on TV, or hold exhibits of their art. The diversity of our students—predominantly African American, Hispanic, Native American, and Hmong, along with refugees from African and Middle Eastern nations—makes their contributions especially eye-opening and important.

From the start, our program has offered not only free tuition and textbooks but also free childcare. We began to hear reports that children of parents in our program started to do better in school, read more, seem more interested in learning. One student said that as he sat at the table to do his homework, his sons would sit with him, all "reading like Dad," including a four-year-old son holding his book upside down. In the past two years, we have added on an Odyssey Junior program, providing enrichment for children of our students on the same night that parents attend classes. Why not have whole families go home talking about vocabulary, art, literature, and other topics?

When we began the UW Odyssey Project in fall 2003, we could not have envisioned how much it would grow. In addition to Odyssey Junior, we now have Onward Odyssey, a series of programs designed for our alumni to help them continue toward degrees and better lives. More than half our budget goes toward keeping graduates of the program in school, supplementing the financial aid they receive. Essential to our high retention rates and our high rate of students continuing on in school (over two-thirds take more college after Odyssey) is the family-like support community we have built around the program. Students feel cared about and supported. Also essential, quite frankly, is money. We rely on grants, institutional support, and individual donors to help defray the costs of tuition, textbooks, notebooks, printer charges, application fees, and other expenses that threaten to shut low-income students out of higher education. We also have actively engaged a large group of community and campus partners—advisers who help steer students into their next classes or help them fill out financial aid forms, public libraries that provide space for our programs, campus departments that offer resources and credits, churches and service clubs that bring us meals, school districts that help train our graduates to work as aides, and businesses that give us discounts.

When an African American mother of three who was homeless for six months when she came to Madison walks across the stage to get her bachelor's degree and then her master's degree from UW–Madison, it feels like a triumph—and one that needs to be replicated everywhere. The UW Odyssey Project serves as a catalyst, a jumpstart, a launching pad—a way to help adults who have gotten off track or were never on the track find a way to start their journeys toward college degrees and better lives. Necessary ingredients for starting a program are respect for "the poor" as equal in their humanity and gifts, commitment to find ways of addressing whole families and their lives outside of class, and creative teaching methods that engage adults with the material in empowering ways.

Earl Shorris is no longer alive, but his work with the Clemente course continues not only in the United States but also abroad (Shorris, 2000, 2013). From Austin, Texas, to Harlem, New York, versions of Earl's course are transforming lives. Some courses, like ours, have diverged from the original model in key ways. The Clemente website (www.clementecourse.org) offers a directory of courses still up and running, as well as directors to contact for more ideas. Earl's (2013) final book, *The Art of Freedom*, has chapters on different versions of the Clemente course, including a chapter called "From Appalachia to Wisconsin" about our Madison program. Programs can occur in homeless shelters, prisons, community centers, and colleges, offering idealistic educators anywhere a chance to fight for social justice by providing equal access to the liberal arts. Although the UW Odyssey Project evolved in a particular context in Madison, Wisconsin, using elements from both the Clemente Course in the Humanities and from Berea College, could aspects of it embolden educators elsewhere to try creative means of engaging adults from underrepresented minorities (Cheney, Newell, Loe, Metcalf, & Newell, 2016)?

Directing the UW Odyssey Project for the past 14 years has restored my faith in the transformative, enduring power of education. An African American grandmother who climbed out of drug addiction and prostitution writes, "Henry David Thoreau said 'You cannot dream yourself into a character: you must hammer and forge yourself into one.' The Odyssey Project helped me hammer and forge myself into the person I was meant to be." A Native American man overcoming alcoholism and discrimination for both his race and sexual orientation comments, "I don't feel lost now. I have a purpose: to educate myself, to break free from the manacles binding my mind. I am a philosopher in training." An African American single father of two rebuilding his life after incarceration calls the program "a life jacket tossed just as I was about to drown in a sea of uncertainty." A refugee from Sudan who received her master's degree in social work from UW–Madison in May 2017 envisions Odyssey as her "passport to higher education and a better life." Hundreds of similar comments, often sparkling with brilliant metaphors, testify to the power of the humanities to break down barriers and change lives (UW Odyssey Project, 2017).

Suggested Cross-References

For more information on concepts and ideas discussed in this article, please see the following articles in the compendium: 1, 2, 4, 6, 7, 9, 10, 11, 12, 13, 15, 17, 19, 22, 23, 24, 25, 26, 33, 34, 35, 37, 42, 43, 44, 49, 51, 52, 54, 57, 60, 65, 66, 67, 60, 70, 71, 74, 75, 76, 78, 79, 80

References

Berea College. (2015). Retrieved from www.berea.edu

Cheney, J., Newell, L. J., Loe, H. S., Metcalf, J., & Newell, B. M. (2016). *Hope, heart, and the humanities: How a free college course is changing lives.* Salt Lake City, UT: University of Utah Press.

Shakespeare, W., & Muir, K. (2013). *Macbeth.* (Original work published in 1606). London: Bloomsbury.

Shorris, E. (2000). *Riches for the poor: The Clemente Course in the Humanities.* New York, NY: Norton.

Shorris, E. (2013). *The art of freedom: Teaching the humanities to the poor.* New York, NY: Norton.

UW Odyssey Project. (2017). Retrieved from. www.odyssey.wisc.edu

15

PROMOTING GENDER EQUITY AND LEADERSHIP AMONG ETHIOPIAN WOMEN IN MEDICINE

Elizabeth Kvach, Mahlet Gebremariam, Fiker Taddesse, and Cynthia Haq

Keywords: Ethiopia, gender equity, higher education, leadership, women

Gender equity, or access to educational and employment opportunities, freedoms, and political representation without discrimination based on gender, is central to human development and achievement of sustainable development goals (SDGs; UNGA, 2015). Gender discrimination has resulted in gender imbalances in the health professional workforce in many countries. This imbalance is notable in countries such as Ethiopia where gender discrimination is widespread with limited opportunities for girls to access higher education (Ethiopian Society, 2008).

In Ethiopia, significant gender inequality persists through widespread discrimination, gender-based violence, and low numbers of women completing higher education (Arnold et al., 2008; Marsh et al., 2009). At Addis Ababa University College of Health Sciences (AAU-CHS), less than 5% of medical faculty were women in 2010 (Kvach et al., 2015). One explanation for this shortage is traditional cultural beliefs that women should fill stereotypical domestic roles, have limited decision-making power, and not hold leadership positions. Influential male leaders with these views are unlikely to promote gender equity. Consequentially, the few women who are in higher education may become disengaged because of exclusion as well as lack of support for seeking leadership positions. Many women express lack of confidence, fear of acceptance, and a need to focus on traditional priorities. Therefore, they have low rates of enrollment and high rates of attrition in higher education. Alternatively, leaders who support gender equity can transform institutional culture and promote inclusion and leadership of female students and faculty.

International interinstitutional collaboration can play a significant role in supporting gender equity efforts through capacity-building for women. The University of Wisconsin (UW) joined the Medical Education Partnership Initiative (MEPI), a multi-institutional, five-year collaboration funded in 2010 by the U.S. government to strengthen the capacity of Ethiopia's health system. This partnership was based on relationships among faculty champions for gender equity promotion in medical education. The leadership of Ethiopian medical schools identified several accomplished Ethiopian women faculty who participated in a two-week intensive fellowship to enhance their leadership skills. The Ethiopian women met with UW women faculty to share stories, build trust, and discuss the challenges of leadership in academic medicine influenced by gender. The curriculum prioritized principles of adult education, including reviewing real-life experiences with gender-related problems that participants had encountered in higher education and restricting the training length to minimize absence from personal responsibilities. Ethiopian participants were challenged to create gender equity action plans for their own institutions.

Several factors positively influenced outcomes of these efforts. First, this initiative was built on evidence from the international development community that addressing gender disparities is crucial for success of other indicators of human development. This produced a mandate to promote gender equity in health profession education in the MEPI grant. Second, UW partners, Ethiopian institutions, and the Ethiopian diaspora had previously worked together on other projects, such as the development of postgraduate medical education training programs. These preexisting relationships built a foundation of trust to tackle the challenging issue of gender equity. Third, female UW faculty were able to offer expertise and share common experiences with female Ethiopian faculty. This created awareness of the global nature of gender discrimination in higher education and leadership, and allowed for creation of mentoring relationships. Lastly, the support of progressive leaders, especially men, was crucial to change at the Ethiopian institutional level. Male leaders were committed to recruiting female faculty to partner with international collaborators for the leadership trainings. Meaningful changes in institutional policy, such as the development of a sexual harassment policy at AAU-CHS, were spearheaded by male and female leaders determined to advance gender equity.

These efforts addressed the gap of women in leadership positions by identifying motivated women faculty and mobilizing their leadership aptitudes and aspirations. One woman became the dean of the medical school at AAU-CHS. The training, adapted to the Ethiopian context, enabled critical thinking and challenged the deep-rooted internalized sexism that contributes to lack of professional self-confidence. Participants were able to interact with U.S. female leaders and envision possibilities for themselves in leadership roles with further mentorship and training. Ethiopian women in leadership positions are role models for those earlier in their careers; these women leaders provide living examples that women can competently manage multiple responsibilities and that capable leadership is an acquired skill not exclusive to men. It gives young female academicians the courage and hope to believe in their own self-worth and achieve their full potential.

Much work needs to be done to sustain and expand efforts to advance equity for all women in Ethiopia. International collaboration should be strengthened for purposes of mentorship and capacity-building in higher education. The aim is to establish numerous training programs for women's empowerment and leadership throughout the nation. Curricula should be developed for students to foster awareness regarding the impact of gender discrimination, how to create gender inclusiveness, and basic leadership skills. Universities could lead the way by establishing and enforcing policies to promote gender equity as essential for productive academic environments; they could set parameters to monitor and evaluate the institutional gender climate. Men and women working together have potential to promote institutional and national legislative changes at all levels. A policy of institutional affirmative action could be considered to create better access to university education for women in Ethiopia. These goals will help pave the way for gender equity and for Ethiopian women to achieve their highest aspirations.

Suggested Cross-References

For more information on concepts and ideas discussed in this article, please see the following articles in the compendium: 6, 11, 14, 17, 23, 25, 33, 35, 37, 39, 44, 49, 57, 58, 60, 65, 66, 75, 78, 80

References

Arnold, D., Gelaye, B., Goshu, M., Berhane, Y., & Williams, M. A. (2008). Prevalence and risk factors of gender-based violence among female college students in Awassa, Ethiopia. *Violence and Victims*, *23*(6), 787–800.

Ethiopian Society of Population Studies. (2008). *Gender inequality and women's empowerment.* Retrieved from http://ethiopia.unfpa.org/drive/Gender.pdf

Kvach, E. K., Desalegn, D., Conniff, J., Tefera, G., Derbew, M. D., & Haq, C. (2015). Promoting gender equity at the College of Health Sciences, Addis Ababa University, Ethiopia. *Ethiopian Medical Journal, 53*(2), 9–16.

Marsh, J., Patel, S., Gelaye, B., Goshu, M., Worku, A., Williams, M. A., & Berhane, Y. (2009). Prevalence of workplace abuse and sexual harassment among female faculty and staff. *Journal of Occupational Health, 51*(4), 314–322.

UNGA, (2015). *Transforming our world: The 2030 agenda for sustainable development,* UN Doc A/RES/70/1. Retrieved http://www.un.org/ga/search/view_doc.asp?symbol=A/RES/70/1&Lang=E

16

LEVELING THE FIELD

Professional Development for Part-Time Employees

Sarah Korpi

Keywords: adjuncts, andragogy, interaction, issues, online instruction, part-time employees, professional development, remote employees

The jobs of tomorrow do not exist today, and globalization, as Hackling (2015) notes, "has resulted in workforces that are increasingly mobile (physically and virtually) both within and between countries" (p. 61). Whereas educators reflect on how they might prepare today's students for tomorrow's jobs, employers are grappling with a different dilemma: their employees are already educated, but their jobs require new competencies. Uniting the need for ongoing, job-focused training with best practices in adult educational pedagogy was the foundation for an innovative professional development program at the University of Wisconsin–Madison.

Theoretical Foundation

The assertion that adults and children learn differently, the premise of Malcolm Knowles's (1970) seminal work on andragogy, continues to serve as the basis for discussions of adult education today. According to Knowles (Knowles, Holton, & Swanson, 2014), adults become ready to learn on a need-to-know basis. Further, they are capable of self-direction, bring with them a multitude of accumulated experiences, and must apply their learning immediately.

Understanding employees as adult learners can and should have a profound impact on how instructional material is developed, packaged, and delivered. As Elliott, Rhoades, Jackson, and Mandernach (2015) discuss, employees' participation in optional professional development is driven primarily by their interest in the topic and scheduling availability.

Initial Orientation and Ongoing Professional Development

The professional development model begins with an online, asynchronous orientation course, which establishes a firm foundation for instructional staff. The orientation course covers topics ranging from job responsibilities to best practices in online pedagogy. Because new staff simultaneously complete the orientation and teach, they are able to put their learning into immediate practice with students. The self-paced nature of the orientation course relies on the instructor's self-direction while learning. The assessments in the orientation course require instructors to combine their experience and expertise in their field with the new course content. Additionally, monthly newsletters, quarterly meetings, and a resource website provide ongoing and timely support and development, remind staff of topics covered in the orientation course, and provide updates to these topics as needed.

Conclusions

The multifaceted training program fits the specific learning needs of adults and allows a network and community to emerge. The website serves as the hub of this community; it is not only an archive of material and a place to find needed information but also a space for discussion. Instructors are able to engage in conversation during the quarterly meetings, and then continue those conversations through an e-mail list or via the website. Participants reported an appreciation for networking opportunities, timely access to information, opportunities for continued learning, and need-based support. The resulting consistencies increased effective student support and allowed instructional staff to focus more intentionally on pedagogical needs.

The community of practice (CoP) that developed out of the training program has proven to be a vital support system for new and veteran instructional staff. As basic staff training needs have been addressed, the need for a space to interact with colleagues emerged. The website, the central hub of the training program, is growing in response to provide a place for instructors to share examples, best practices, and time-saving measures that support the learning needs of students. The structure of the training program and resulting CoP is adaptable for a variety of fields.

Suggested Cross-References

For more information on concepts and ideas discussed in this article, please see the following articles in the compendium: 4, 6, 21, 24, 25, 26, 31, 35, 39, 47, 51, 53, 58, 59, 62, 74, 75, 76, 78, 79

References

Elliott, M., Rhoades, N., Jackson, C. M., & Mandernach, B. J. (2015). Professional development: Designing initiatives to meet the needs of online faculty. *Journal of Educators Online, 12*(1), 160–188.

Hackling, M. W. (2015). Think piece: Preparing today's children for the workplaces of tomorrow: The critical role of STEM education. *International Journal of Innovation in Science and Mathematics Education (formerly CAL-laborate International), 23*(3), 61–63.

Knowles, M. S. (1970). *The modern practice of adult education: Andragogy versus pedagogy*. New York, NY: Association Press.

Knowles, M. S., Holton III, E. F., & Swanson, R. A. (2014). *The adult learner: The definitive classic in adult education and human resource development*. New York: Routledge.

GLOSSARY

Glossary terms provide definitions, examples, or explanations for use by compendium readers.

Ability: along with similar terms such as *aptitude, experience, capacity, talent, mastery, preparation*, and *acquired proficiency*, type and extent of mental, emotional, and physical capability to perform.

Aboriginal: along with similar concepts such as original, indigenous, first nation, and early people, populations with characteristics and cultures of people who long ago lived in an area that was later occupied by people from another culture and language.

Access: awareness of and lack of barriers to opportunities such as learning activities for adults.

Achievement: progress and related assessment procedures for comparing indicators of current proficiency or performance, in relation to standards or expectations, as indications of preparation and progress; estimates of initial and current proficiency (for a participant, teacher, or other stakeholder) can help evaluate and report progress.

Action: interactions and performance in many adult roles, including efforts by adult learners to apply benefits from participation in educational activities.

Activity: when referring to adult participants in an educational activity, a sequence of program procedures, intended to stimulate, guide, and sustain a learning process and outcomes that can be guided by the learner and other people and materials, to assess and enhance proficiency and actual performance.

Administration: various tasks intended to encourage members of an organization or group to agree on desirable objectives and to contribute to their achievement, including provision of coordination and resources.

Adult: in relation to educational activities for adults, a person, usually aged 16 or older, with some adult roles related to work, family, voting, drinking, driving, and usually, completion of full-time preparatory education.

Advocacy: individual and collective efforts in support of an organization, activity, or goal.

Aesthetic: relate to creativity and the arts, but can refer to similar features of any type of performance or result.

Affective: a domain of living, learning, and performing composed of feelings, needs, values, emotions, inclinations, and attitudes that, along with the cognitive (knowledge) and psychomotor (skill) domains, constitute proficiency and enhanced performance.

Affluence: relative abundance regarding levels of economic wealth, material resources, and financial means, but may include nonmaterial resources.

Africa: a global region, specifically a continent between the Mediterranean and the South Pole, and between the Atlantic and Indian oceans, that includes many countries, languages, and traditions.

Alignment: a desirable match or connection between several aspects, such as learner and teacher, or provider and potential participants, or provider budget and financial support.

Analysis: typically, explaining how things work, including describing major parts and how they fit together; usually part of inquiry for research, evaluation, and strategic planning.

Andragogik/Andragogy: a label for the scientific discipline studying lifelong and lifewide adult learning and education; including education and learning of adults in various forms, *Andragogik* is used as a header for places of systematic reflections, parallel to other academic headers (i.e., biology, medicine, or physics).

Andragogy: an old European term about a scholarly discipline to help adults learn, and a term popularized by Malcolm Knowles about practitioners who plan and conduct many types of educational activities that are responsive to adult learners.

Apprenticeship: a traditional form of individualized teaching and learning, largely related to work, that is similar to coaching, internship, preceptorship, and mentoring.

Art and Science: combinations of mastery and proficiencies related to educational activities for adults, such as evidence-based, tested, and organized guidelines, in combination with creative interactions with people and materials that are responsive to the complex interplay of standards and procedures by multiple stakeholders (participants, teachers, coordinators) with diverse characteristics, aspirations, values, and situational influences.

Arts-Based: various educational opportunities for adults, for which participation and appreciation of creative arts is central.

Asia: a large geographic and population region of the world, west of the Pacific Ocean, east of the Indian Ocean, and north of Australia that includes languages and cultures related to China, Japan, Korea, and India, and many countries with various political, economic, and social traditions and connections.

Aspiration: a desire to pursue, create, achieve, or embrace a tangible or intangible goal, experience, or connection that participants and other program stakeholders can have, express, and pursue individually or collectively as a shared vision.

Assessment: many types of analysis of needs, aspirations, accomplishments, and relationships, such as personal discernment, as well as program decisions related to educational needs assessment, program satisfaction, and stakeholder cooperation.

Association: membership organizations, including for educators of adults, which along with experience and formal preparation, can contribute to educator's proficiency and networking.

Attitudes: a popular synonym for the affective domain that can be estimated, as a preference or feeling about a fact or condition, and may influence perceptions, interpretations, and actions without being outwardly expressed, which can be more influential on actions than knowledge.

Autonomy: a degree of independence by a person, group, or organization based on choice regarding goals and procedures.

Basic Education: educational programs for adults that emphasize responsive learning activities such as literacy, numeracy, vocational education, life skills, and completion of secondary education requirements, and sometimes preparation for citizenship, occupations, and higher education.

Benefits: results or outcomes of a process in the form of tangible or intangible assistance or contribution to personal or societal well-being for a person, family, group, organization, community, society, or the environment.

Budgeting: planning and implementing decisions about receipt and expenditure of money and time to achieve intended results and benefits.

Capability: the extent of being able, and having one or more mental, physical, and emotional attributes sufficient for desired performance and actual context or setting, with a combination of personal and situational influences.

Capital: can refer to human capital, related to personal resources for learning and living, as well as economic capital for providers and enterprises.

Care: along with terms such as *love* and *empathy*, positive feelings about self, others, environment, and objects of interest and concern, in which the purpose, process, and results of interaction can be mutually beneficial.

Cascade: suggests a series of transitions, pools, or levels, among which material resources or ideas are shared with each successive level; cascade of learning refers to a sequence of people who share and assist other people to learn, who each model and facilitate exchanges of content and process that continue the cascade.

Case: a specific instance, such as a case example for inquiry, or case study for analysis and learning about how things work in a context.

Change: conditions related to an increase, decrease, or modification of the direction, location, or position of a person, group, organization, community, or society that may have a clear source or direction, exchange, benefit, or compensation, but in relation to lifelong learning is sometimes assumed to potentially include desirable directions, outcomes, and compensations.

Character: a general term for desirable personal adult qualities, such as creativity, dependability, honestly, empathy, cooperation, and wisdom, which may be criteria for selection of effective educators, and intended outcomes for participants.

Citizen: typically, one or more adult residents of an area, who may or may not be eligible voters.

City: along with cities, refers to a large community, district, or metropolitan region that can be the service area for provision of learning activities by adults, such as learning cities.

Coaching Leadership: an approach to leadership defined as a way of leading that enables people to resolve challenging problems, improve personal and professional performance, and access latent potential in order to develop and improve talent.

Cognitive: a domain consisting of ways of knowing, including awareness and judgment, which for human learning includes the process of perceiving, interpreting, remembering, accessing, transmitting, and using knowledge for being and functioning in the world (for pre-adult teaching and instruction, mastery, transmission, and acquisition of knowledge is sometimes considered the central function of education).

Collaboration: a form of cooperation and partnership, typically includes agreements on mutually beneficial exchanges with a consortium that has a more formal and enduring arrangement.

Collection: may refer to acquisition of money or cooperation, but for research and evaluation, includes obtaining data to be analyzed and reported.

Communication: a general concept about interactions among people in which senders and receivers use various means of exchanging information and feelings, such as observation, demonstration, conversation, discussion, body language, public events, and various combinations of media, including radio, television, computer, and social media, from which adults selectively use and interpret based on their values and preferred communication style; these complex communications dynamics occur within learning activities, and in the local, national, and international context.

Community: includes people in a geographic or interest area who are connected regarding intentions, interests, policies, transactions, and exchanges, and for educators of adults, may include community of practice, learning community, digital community, global community, community center, organization development, and community development, each of which depends on personal beliefs about shared values, beneficial exchanges, collective benefits, procedural guidelines, and acceptance of diversity.

Community Development: includes an educational process for adult members of any community, typically involving specialists who facilitate a process that includes participation by adults who are representative of various aspects of the community, who help analyze community strengths, weaknesses, opportunities, and threats, to gain understanding and support for shared commitment to goals and procedures for progress.

Comparative: analysis of similarities and differences to enhance understanding, which can be used for international, national, or local comparative analysis of educational programs for adults; comparative analysis procedures also occur in related professional fields and scholarly disciplines, which can include revelation of deeper insights about local dynamics that were taken for granted.

Concepts: in most compendium article content, consist of explanations and examples to help readers understand the nature of the content, which could enhance their performance.

Conclusions: findings, results, and implications from research, evaluation, and program analysis.

Congruous: agreement, harmony, correspondence, appropriate, suitable.

Connections: readers can use multiple connections to navigate from article to related article by use of keywords in the table of contents and index, links among numbers of related articles, and a compendium article that explains procedures and examples, to enable readers to enhance their self-directed inquiry of topics related to their experience and interests.

Context: a general term related to a person, organization, or nation as an open system, which refers to broader interactions with societal, political, economic, and demographic influences and interactions.

Continuing Professional Education: a lifelong education process for professionals to provide learning activities for the continual development and advancement of professional expertise to assure quality in professional services provided to clients.

Continuity: in contrast to change, entails stability that may seem desirable or undesirable but has elements of persistence, duration, connections, coherence, and predictability that enables a person, group, organization, community, and society to function when making plans, decisions, choices and investments of time, effort, and resources in relation to desirable priorities and goals; for lifelong learning, elements of continuity may be especially important as a stable platform for dealing with major changes.

Continuum: a series or sequence of longitudinal actions, interactions, and relationships that focus on continuity and sometimes progression, such as connections among stages of professional development, or annual stages of external funding of a provider organization.

Cooperation: includes interactions among people, groups, organizations, or associations that lead to satisfactory and continued relationships.

Coordination: occurs when program coordinators and organizers help adults learn, along with attracting and sustaining participants, teachers, and resources.

Course: is a way of organizing content and teaching/learning activities as a sequence of units or parts, and may include a record of participation and evidence from assessment.

Creativity: the ability and process of artistic, scientific, and interpersonal contributions that add value through individual and collective originality and innovation that sometimes entails patent or copyright protection for creative people and the innovative process; for educators of adults, and collective efforts in the arts and sciences by various helping professions, contributions can apply to adult learners, people who help them learn, educational materials, and program stakeholders generally.

Criteria (for manuscipts): indicators included in the website explanation of a framework and basis for drafting each article that served as suggested criteria as the manuscript was being drafted and revised, with assistance from a consulting editor (brevity, brief title, keywords, relevance, examples, concepts, influences, implications, and references).

Critical Perspective: use of critical thinking to analyze societal influences instead of taking them for granted, and to advocate reform if deemed warranted.

Culture: a combination of beliefs, practices, results, and relationships shared among members of a group, program, family, workplace, community, association, nation, civilization, and subculture; the term *cultural* can apply to organizations such as libraries and museums that provide resources and assistance.

Data: facts, figures, and other information that can be specified for analysis in reports, research, and evaluation as a basis for conclusions and recommendations.

Decisions: important choices, commitments, and plans by educators of adults, which can entail connections among concepts explained in articles from multiple parts of the compendium.

Decolonization: a process of withdrawing or overthrowing a condition of being colonized.

Design: a general to very detailed plan, pattern, or template to guide creation of a work of art, piece of equipment, activity, or educational program.

Development: an evolving process and result of gradual growth, change, extension, differentiation, and modification to enhance capacity and make manifest emerging opportunities, which can apply to physical, mental, attitudinal, and societal characteristics of any person including stakeholders for educational programs for adults; because of variation regarding circumstances, roles, opportunities, deterrents, relationships, values, and relative priorities the life cycle process of growth and decline can include transitions in functioning and outlook; similar influences and stages can occur for persons, families, groups, organizations, communities, and societies.

Digital: computer-based technology and communication methods; electronic technology that generates, stores, and processes data.

Disability: any physical, emotional, mental, or social limitation that can impair or restrict a person's capability and performance, which may depend on personal and organizational efforts to minimize restrictions.

Discipline: regarding learning and education, refers to structure and mastery in a field of study, practice, and advancement.

Discrepancy: can refer to a gap between current and desired proficiency or performance.

Discrimination: once meant making accurate informed distinctions, but now usually refers to negative value judgments, typically without explicit criteria.

Diverse: people, groups, communities, and societies differ in various ways regarding forms or characteristics, and for adult learning opportunities, this includes each learner's many characteristics that influence their readiness, participation, progress, satisfaction, and uses of the process and outcomes of learning activities; diversity includes group and population characteristics; variations among educators of adults from various countries who use the compendium reflect many types of organizations that help provide learning opportunities for adults, who vary in experience, abilities, and interests.

Economic: use of money or the equivalent for exchange of property, goods, and services in which economic indicators monitor trends and extent of financial exchanges for a family, organization, nation state, or confederation (e.g., the European Union).

Educator(s): practitioners and scholars who help plan, conduct, administer, and evaluate learning activities, who constitute educators of adults.

Elders: similar to seniors and third age, includes older men and women in a family, community, or organization who have experience and values desired by younger people, related to roles and relationships that entail advising, judging, and inspiring.

e-Leadership: leadership via electronic media; it is particularly important during the information age, which engages increasing numbers of employees in the application of technology as a routine aspect of their work responsibilities.

Empathy: understanding, attitudes, and caring about the feelings and conditions of others.

Empower: to help people to become more effective and use their abilities.

Engage: active participation, exchanges, and interactions with other people or groups, which can result in mutually beneficial exchanges.

Enterprise: a general term for various types of public or private organizations, such as government agency, military installation, business organization, or industrial plant, in which human resource development staff and departments arrange learning activities for staff members to collaborate with other provider organizations.

Ethics: formulation and use of a system of moral values and principles of conduct by persons or groups, which can serve as content for learning activities and guide procedures for provider organizations.

Evaluation: judging and assessing the worth of something; for evaluation of educational programs for adults, includes explicit criteria and other standards of evaluation procedures.

Events: a general term for related activities, which include aspects of educational procedures and outcomes.

Evidence: one basis for decisions in helping professional fields of practice, using tested or organized knowledge as a basis for planning and evaluating performance; another basis for practice is evaluation and conclusions from professional experience generally explaining how things work in context.

Excellence: a concept and standard for judging performance that includes both process and results for participants, teachers, coordinators, programs, and providers.

Exchange: transfer of values, goods, or services among persons, groups, organizations, or providers; entails cooperation, collaboration, and interactions in educational activities and various adult role relationships, which can be beneficial exchanges, with the benefits depending on the perception of the people engaged in the exchanges; the effect of exchanges can be complementary, in which each member learns and benefits.

Experience: various types of role performance and related plans, decisions, and rehearsals that learning activities are intended to enhance, related to the participants and other educational program stakeholders who have engaged in previous, current, and future activities; individually, cooperatively, or in community; related to experiential learning.

Explanation: brief and substantive analysis and report of major systemic features and relationships (logic model) that characterizes a program, contribution, resource, policy, process, outcome, or influence, in a form that helps program stakeholders understand how things work, which can contribute to stakeholder interests, cooperation, contributions, and program excellence.

Extension: a traditional term for continuing higher education programs and public service activities that are provided at times and locations that make them accessible to adult part-time students, in contrast to on-campus courses for full-time students.

Feedback: when people and organization members receive information about the process and results of their activity that they can use for plans, adjustments, activities, and decisions; such feedback in the teaching–learning transaction helps the teacher (coordinator, provider, and evaluator) modify the learning activities, and positive feedback is especially important for positive reinforcement and guidance for participant progress and assistance.

Feelings: emotions, attitudes, needs, and preferences that are combined with other parts of the affective domain that guides people's impulses and reactions such as love, anger, hatred, pleasure, resentment, and joy; educators of adults can estimate learner's feelings by body language, expression, actions, and intentions as guides for use of encouragement, mentoring, procedures, and materials to facilitate participant progress, benefits, and improved performance.

Feminist: attitudes, actions, and influences on behalf of recognition, rights, activities, and relationships pertaining to the equality of the sexes.

Funding: for a provider organization, includes sources and extent of money or similar financial support for educational programs or contributions.

Future: oriented concepts emphasize past trends, analyses, decisions, and forecasts that contribute to choices and actions that occur in later years.

Global: international connections and influences on ideas, programs, environment, culture, media, economic, and political systems.

Governance: in contrast to ruling, which can be despotic or arbitrary, a desirable process of having influence over policies and procedures of an organization for the good of individuals and the collective.

Guide: includes various individualized ways of assisting adults regarding their exploration, inquiry, learning, discovery, growth, rehabilitation, recovery, mastery, proficiency, and performance.

Health: can refer broadly to conditions of a person, group, organization, ecosystem, nation, or region, ranging from robust to damaged, which reflect positive influences, such as prudent conservation, prevention, development, judgment, balance, aspiration, wisdom, rest, and relaxation, as well as negative influences, such as wasting, degradation, disease, illness, injury, neglect, and aggression.

Helping Professions: occupations and vocations that emphasize nurturing and assistance, such as education, health, and counseling, which can contribute to a cascade of learning where inquiry and learning that contributes to the effectiveness of a helping professional becomes a desirable central quality for the people who benefit and are served, such as students, patients, and clients.

Higher Education: various colleges and universities, along with other post-secondary educational institutions.

History: the methods, process, results, and reports from use of procedures, concepts, records, analysis, synthesis, cross validation, and interpretation to help explain past trends, influences, and results; related to a person, group, organization, community, and professional fields.

Holistic: a comprehensive concept that includes consideration of the whole as more than the sum of the parts of a person, group, organization, nation, or world.

Humanities: a number of scholarly fields such as language, literature, art, music, history, and philosophy in which teachers and students study and share understanding and appreciation that includes subjective and creative aspects of human activities, interactions, and accomplishments.

Identity: usually refers to a person's sense of self, such as a unity and persistence of personality that reflects multiple personal and situational influences; participants sometimes report that a more positive sense of self (e.g., self-confidence or direction) was a major benefit of educational participation.

Impaired: some part of a person that has been limited due to either a birth condition or an injury.

Implications: suggested as conclusions of a compendium article for comparative analysis and local guidelines and use in diverse settings along with a few important selected accessible references to publications that contain greater details; a list of implications in a publication or report typically connects the main conclusions with suggestions for continued applications.

Inclusive: people or activities part of a broader category.

Independence: options for people or activities.

Indicator: usually a brief amount of information that is relatively easy to monitor as an estimate of complex trends and relationships, such as economic and social indicators.

Influences: regarding personal and organizational performance, typically reflect combinations of personal and situational influences to be understood and addressed.

Informal: a category of adult learning activities where participants arrange without a provider organization.

Information-Seeking: varies in ways in which people pay attention and inquire; the extent and content of information seeking reflects their concerns; types of information seeking include: observation, conversation, electronic media, and reading, with word-of-mouth a widespread means, and the use of reading positively associated with educational level.

Inquiry: a way to creatively use scholarly disciplines to discover new insight; each discipline (history, philosophy, sociology, psychology, political science, or economics) uses theoretical, conceptual, and experimental procedures to answer questions; educators of adults can use both multidisciplinary inquiry and findings from organized knowledge; program stakeholders can use research and evaluation concepts for transcendent performance.

Interactive: regarding discussion groups, usually includes informal group activities in which members interact; the process can be enhanced by leader guidance and member experience and interactions.

Interpretation: part of research, evaluation, counseling, and other professional assistance after pertinent information has been collected and analyzed for the purpose of conclusions and recommendations.

Interprofessional: regarding learning and performance, occurs when members of two or more professions collaborate to provide coordinated assistance to the person being served.

Interview: a way to acquire information from people for purposes of mentoring, teaching, planning, evaluation, research, and administration.

Issues: usually concern important topics about which there are various perspectives that deserve consideration, analysis, reflection, and action.

Know: along with knowing and knowledge, part of the cognitive domain based on observation, analysis, validation, and reflection, in contrast to the affective domain composed of attitudes, emotions, and feelings, and the psychomotor domain focused on skills and performance.

Latin America: a region in the southern Western hemisphere composed of Central and South America between the Atlantic and Pacific Oceans that includes many distinctive countries, cultures, languages, and social, economic, and political systems.

Leader: along with lead and leading, a process that can apply to a teacher, coordinator, or other stakeholder who helps achieve progress with and through other people by encouraging them to contribute to the achievement of shared goals.

Learning Informally: occurs from observation, conversation, and casual media use everywhere throughout life; formal learning occurs in credit-related programs conducted by faculty and others in higher education and other learning contexts; nonformal learning can include other organized learning activities such as human resource development activities in enterprises, learning activities in community agencies, associations, e-learning programs, and self-directed learning projects; typical ingredients include objectives, content, process, practice, and feedback; rationales for helping adults learn how to learn have emphasized decisions by participants.

Lifelong: related to learning, usually refers to all types of formal, nonformal, and informal learning, and educational activities for adults.

Link (article links or cross-references): connections between adult learning activities and decisions that typically entail multiple relevant concepts and topics; in the compendium, there are many links to help readers use self-directed inquiry to discover useful connections.

Literacy: part of basic education for adults and adult functional literacy includes the ability to observe, listen, speak, read, and write regarding language, numeracy, and basic tasks related to family, health, work, finance, and citizenship.

Longitudinal: an ongoing activity that can be assessed with time series data for planning, research, evaluation, and counseling purposes.

Map: along with mapping, portrays connections among topics of interest to guide travelers in an unfamiliar domain; creating, portraying, or using roadmap content entails experience, study, and understanding of a domain of interests to guide decisions about connections; the compendium website matrix provides connections among concepts to create a preliminary map of parts, topics, subtopics, and concepts, to encourage proposals for articles about any brief and substantive topics of benefit to educators of adults to guide their discovery of connections among topics relevant to their program decisions.

Market: an economic concept about exchanges of value such as connections, communication, and cooperation between an educational program for adults and potential participants.

Mastery: effective performance requiring intent, time, practice, feedback, persistence, and encouragement to achieve a satisfactory level of ability; expert levels may require years of preparation.

Meaning: a goal for some adults who engage in learning activities as a part of their active search for fulfilment.

Media: a general term that refers to communication forms such as print, radio, films, television, computers, and social media.

Members: people connected with an association, enterprise, organization, or group, some of whom share an interest as participants in learning activities.

Memory: storage, retention, recall, and reconstruction of knowledge, attitudes, and skills.

Mentoring: a personalized way of helping adults learn about various roles and interests; typical features related to a mentor or coach include voluntary agreements on arrangements for assistance, mentor provision of guidance and encouragement, and focus on mentee performance.

Methods: available to educators of adults and the adult learners they assist, with a great variety of teaching and learning methods available to select and sequence types of learning activities that fit program content and objectives, along with participant experiences and aspirations.

Microaggressions: comprised of environmental, verbal, or nonverbal insults or slights that communicate negative, aggressive, and disparaging comments to targeted persons based on their membership with a specific group (e.g., differences in race, gender, sexual orientation, culture, and professional role), which can negatively impact workplace operations.

Middle East: a diverse region between Africa, Mediterranean, Europe, India, and Russia that includes various countries, traditions, and systems with long disputed borders of countries.

Millennials: individuals born between 1982 and 2003.

Mixed-Economy: a combination of public and private enterprise that influences policies and procedures for production, consumption, regulation, finance, and coordination.

Model: includes many forms of electronic, two- and three-dimensional simplified portrayals of more complex objects, concepts, or relationships of people and ecosystems that can be very effective simulations for learning purposes.

Movement: efforts by adults to influence policies and societal arrangements in an area by demonstrating the extent of support for desired changes; educators of adults sometimes assist with movements that are aligned with provider goals regarding desirable social change.

Multicultural: a concept that includes interactions from people who collectively may have two or more cultural traditions that can lead to learning and change, which for some may be an educational objective.

Multidisciplinary: perspectives and conclusions result from a combination of methods, conclusions, and implications from multiple scholarly fields; there are specialties related to education of adults, such as anthropology, sociology, economics, history, philosophy, psychology, neuroscience, demography, and geography.

Narrative: may be an oral or written message that might be published or only shared among members of a group.

Needs: a concept used by educators of adults to explain motives by categorizing and characterizing a combination of personal and situational conditions that are important to adults, such as needs for achievement, affiliation, and intimacy; educators of adults also assess adults' educational needs and preferences to guide provision of responsive learning activities.

Networking: being with other people with similar interests to enhance careers and relate to the purposes of the provider program; it is one reason program participants attend learning groups.

Nonformal: various types of adult learning activities, except formal (continuing higher education programs) and informal (spontaneous learning activities that adults engage in without a provider organization).

Nonprofit: groups and organizations that have service and educational purposes that often depend upon volunteers and contributions.

North America: a region in the Western hemisphere between the Atlantic and Pacific Oceans that includes the United States and Canada.

Objectives: specified intended outcomes from learning activities that can include both content and ways in which the learner can demonstrate progress and level of mastery; for some adult learning activities related to performance, it is an early activity to ensure agreement on learning objectives, to guide progress, provide ongoing feedback, and assess results.

Obtain: a general term regarding acquisition of cooperation from people, use of facilities, and purchase of materials and equipment.

Online: regarding distance education, use of electronic or computer connections between one or more adult learners, instructor, and other participants.

Opportunities: for adult learning, can result from leadership by effective educators of adults who understand systemic relationships among acquisition of people and resources, process of teaching and coordination, outcomes, results, and feedback regarding relationships within an organizational and societal context.

Oppression: a condition of people who are denied basic human rights and other freedoms.

Oral: communication, traditions, and culture that depend heavily on speaking, listening, remembering, and observing (in contrast to extensive use of reading and writing by more formally educated adults) is a distinguishing feature of ancient civilizations; oral communication is also central for a substantial portion of adults who seldom read but depend mainly on word-of-mouth and electronic media for information to guide their decisions.

Organizational Consultant: an adviser to educational activity, helping organization members improve organizational functioning.

Outcomes: in adult learning activities, outcomes take various forms, tend to be cumulative with lifelong connections to related activities, and sometimes have results beyond achieving program objectives; examples of program outcomes include participants who discover new opportunities, benefits for people in roles related to a participant, and connections with other members of an organization or community.

Outreach: one of many terms that refer to connections between higher education institutions and other organizations, and adults in their service area they would like to serve.

Participant: along with participation and participatory, usually diverse adults as they engage in intentional learning activities in addition to performing their typical adult roles and who are especially interested in relevant learning activities; they often want to use enhanced capabilities in their family, local organization, occupation, and community; participation rates are highest for adults during young adulthood, when they are experiencing multiple role changes, and those who have higher educational levels, greater affluence, or interactions with other adult learners, and who often have higher aspirations.

Parts: the compendium parts (learners, teaching, leadership, inquiry) are each composed of articles that reflect the compendium matrix, with the identical content from each part published as a separate print volume for readers mainly interested in concepts and examples related to that part.

Performance: can be enhanced by learning activities related to role performance; lifelong, lifewide, and life-deep learning activities can be for a more coherent life in society and the environment, and for a more unified sense of self and personal values; assessment of performance includes situational expectations, demands and constraints, personal commitments, and capability to include connections beyond personal achievements that are affected by external influences.

Personal: a singular adult, rather than a group, organization, or collective.

Plan: along with planning, curriculum plan, program planning, making decisions about goals and procedures to guide educational and administrative activities and priorities, including cooperation and resources.

Policy: sources may include legislation or more formal agreements that guide decisions by provider organizations, or educators.

Popular: referring to culture, interests, and activities such as communication and entertainment available to the general public.

Power: economic, political, institutional, collective, and charismatic sources that influence policies, priorities, resource allocations, and decisions, including organizational and legal charters and bylaws that may be designed to limit external interference.

Praxis: a concept about the dynamic interactions that can occur among three elements of a learning experience: dialogue, reflection, and action; praxis can be initiated by a teacher, participants, external influences, or an issue, and it can be connected with concerns about personal, organizational, and social change.

Priority: regarding position or setting, includes ranking of importance based on values and previous experience to guide attention to first things first; for educators of adults, values clarification, ranking criteria, and allocation of resources are examples of setting and using priorities for policy-making and decision-making.

Privilege: having or enjoying one or more benefits because of characteristics, status, or category.

Problem-Solving: solving a problem includes understanding a problem or uncertainty, consideration of alternative solutions, selection, and trial of a preferred solution.

Process: a general concept about activities, interactions, and materials for using inputs to achieve outcomes; systemic models for proposals, plans, programs, implementation, and evaluation typically include inputs, process, intended and actual outcome, contexts, and feedback.

Profession: along with professionalization and professional development, characteristics, privileges, and responsibilities of occupations that entail substantial preparation and related features of a continuum of career-long education and enhancement for performance due to changing conditions and expectations.

Professor: a title for college and university faculty members, teachers, and scholars.

Proficiency: along with proficiencies, combinations of knowledge, skills, and attitudes that in combination and enhanced can contribute to excellence and improve performance during and beyond participation in an educational activity, which can be assessed regarding levels (minimal, optimal, maximal) in contrast to a similar concept in preparatory education of minimal or basic competency.

Program: a term or concept used by educators of adults about planning, conducting, and evaluating a series of intentional learning activities; transparent, collaborative, mutually beneficial program relationships among stakeholders can contribute to learning and enhanced performance by each stakeholder.

Project: a general term regarding an activity that includes proposal, plan, implementation, ongoing evaluation feedback and use, outcomes, and reporting, which can focus on teaching learning, provider organization development, collaboration, or pilot efforts and is sometimes characterized as an iterative process of successive approximations.

Proposal: a request for cooperation and support.

Protégé: a learner assisted by a mentor, master, or coach.

Provider: organizations, groups, associations, or people with commitment, resources, and image who are central to planning, conducting, and arranging for program resources and activities.

Publications: in various print and electronic forms (e.g., reports, newsletters, journals, books, and handbooks), can enhance educators' effectiveness and their awareness and use of learning materials to benefit adult participants and the educator's own performance.

Quality: a term used to define desirable features of performance, educational activities, and life so that learning opportunities can provide ways to encourage participants to analyze and reflect on those high-quality features that are deemed desirable.

Reasons: the actions and explanations that people give to characterize their views and preferences; educators of adults sometimes ask potential or actual program participants why they would or actually do engage in learning activities; there are also more predictive ways to estimate reasons, and the intent to act.

Recognition: takes many forms to acknowledge or celebrate contributions, performance, and accomplishments of participants, stakeholders, benefactors, and the people who help adults learn and provide program leadership.

Region: the area within a country, the commuting area of a large city, or a continent or number of adjacent countries.

Relevance: perceived connections between the interests of a person or an organization and potential images, ideas, contributions, or activities.

Renewal: can apply to people, relationships, or organizations that can enhance their functioning as a result of commitment and assistance such as analysis of strengths, weaknesses, opportunities, and threats (SWOT).

Report: oral or written information about an activity, performance, progress, project, research, or evaluation analysis.

Research: a general term for many specific forms of inquiry and action research by scholars and practitioners designed to review and understand concepts and procedures that can help answer and explain questions of interest; sources of information may include other people, library and archival collections of print and electronic materials, general procedures to search pertinent databases, and experimental studies to analyze quantitative data or detailed comparative analysis of qualitative case examples.

Resources: a general category of resources that includes people, ideas, assistance, funding, facilities use, collaboration, and voluntary contributions; program coordinators and administrators may use systemic models that include acquisition and allocation of resources for throughput/processes, including retention, which contribute to outcomes and feedback regarding such transactions in the program context.

Responsibility: being dependable and accountable regarding commitments and expectations related to resources, preparation, activities, people, collaboration, reporting, and goal achievement, and can apply to participants, teachers, coordinators, and administrators; related to educational activities and the provider organization.

Responsive: taking into account stakeholder experience, preferences, conditions, and influences, which is especially important for sustained cooperation by participants.

Self-Direction: occurs for some learning and activities for adults that emphasize the importance of participants having major responsibility to help guide selection of objectives, interpretation of content, reflection on assumptions, engagement in learning activities, and evaluation of progress.

Self-Efficacy: the concept that an adult's sense of self includes understanding the extent and ways in which one can influence features of one's life and situation and make a difference in how things work.

Senior: similar to retirees, senior citizens, older adults, and elders.

Skills: a psychomotor domain in the taxonomy of educational objectives related to physical performance, but sometimes skill is used as a synonym of performance, in contrast to knowledge' proficiency and performance are the results of enhanced skills, combined with knowledge and attitudes; there are various ways to demonstrate, estimate, and assess learner's current and potential skills.

Social Justice: equitable procedures that result in similar opportunities and treatment regardless of personal characteristics.

Southern African Development Community (SADC): countries that are identified as representatives both geographically and politically of southern Africa; the countries include Angola, Botswana, Democratic Republic of Congo, Lesotho, Madagascar, Malawi, Mauritius, Mozambique, Namibia, Seychelles, South Africa, Swaziland, Tanzania, Zambia, and Zimbabwe; the languages include English, which is spoken in the majority of the countries; French; and Portuguese.

Staff Development: learning opportunities for members of enterprises and organizations.

Stakeholders: people in various roles associated with planning, conducting, and assessing learning opportunities for adults, including adult participants, program teachers and coordinators, evaluators, provider organization administrators, funders, and policymakers.

Stereotypes: simplified and incomplete cognitive schemas that characterize a person, group, organization, or society that can be accurate, distorted, or false; one potential benefit of lifelong learning is to help participants replace false stereotypes with more accurate and constructive characterizations.

Strategic Planning: a process for developing, implementing, and evaluating long-term (3 to 10 year) plans for improving organizational performance; typically includes stakeholders related to an educational program, provider organizations, a process of planning that entails analysis of strengths, weaknesses, opportunities, and threats, and using the engagement process and conclusions to enhance the program.

Substantive: referring to ideas, organized explanations that include evidence, relevance, and rationale.

Support: a general concept that includes contributions of money and time by volunteers.

Systemic: referring to models, including logic models, includes relationships among inputs of resources, process, or throughputs; intended and actual outcomes; contexts; and feedback that together contribute to understanding of such relationships to guide planning, decisions, improvements, evaluation, and results.

Taxonomy: usually hierarchically organized with a broader category defined and explained by the contents of subcategories, which for the compendium parts, articles, and concepts (and a taxonomic table of contents), enables readers to use their experience and interests to explore connections among topics that are relevant to their local programs, in part by navigating among articles, grouped by sections, topics, and subtopics.

Teachers: people who help adults learn in organizations, large and small groups, and individually, including use of technology, who are referred to as instructors, guides, presenters, professors, and mentors.

Team: people interacting on behalf of a shared purpose.

Technology: used by educators of adults and in the media, with various forms, including computers, educational materials, models, and simulations to enhance learning, access, practice, and improve performance.

Title: as used in the compendium, may refer to the entire compendium, a separate print volume of a part of the compendium, and of an article, and may be referred to by a brief phrase about the content of an article following the article number to help a reader to select a related article to read.

Topic: usually a collection of related concepts, examples, influences, and procedures that serve as units of study or a selection of print or electronic publications or an aspect of a presentation or discussion.

Transaction: examples of exchanges of special interest to educators of adults include mutually beneficial exchanges between a mentor and a protégé, the teaching learning transaction, and beneficial organizational collaboration; especially for cooperation by stakeholders from various countries and types of provider organizations, use of comparative analysis can contribute to cooperation and sustainability of such partnerships.

Transactional Leader: views the relationship with followers as based on an exchange involving the leader giving followers what they want in return for the attainment of prescribed goals.

Transcendent: understanding and performance by educators of adults based on evidence and practice-based proficiencies that are beyond routine performance, limited personal experience and perceptions.

Transformation: types of educational activities for adults that emphasize consciousness-raising regarding the extent and ways in which societal influences help shape an adult's understanding and expectations.

Transformational Leader: views the relationship with followers in terms of commitment and motivation.

Trend: a way of expressing a longitudinal series of events, activities, and interpretations that enhance understanding of their relationships and implications, compared with only knowing about the separate parts of the series; educators can use trends to explain adult development, organizational changes, and societal influences, for both understanding and prediction.

Understanding: personal comprehension, agreement among people, or the basis for agreement to cooperate.

Urban: the urban context represents the social and environmental situations that inform the lived experiences of individuals, groups, and communities that reside in densely populated cities and surrounding areas; these everyday experiences differ for adult learners based on their sociodemographic characteristics, income and socioeconomic standing, occupation, and other factors.

Utopian: models of communities are between utopian and dystopian models because the utopian perspective recognizes human flaws and aspirations and emphasizes societal arrangements to gradually enhance personal and social well-being, quality of life and relationships, prudent use of resources, and a healthy ecosystem.

Value: a relative ranking of qualities that can reflect multiple unexamined or expressed positive and negative values for which reflection and discernment can help clarify, analyze, and guide conflict resolution efforts, and potentially contribute to greater understanding of a personal or collective hierarchy of values to guide goal setting, decisions, and actions.

Virtual Reality: the use of technology to allow for interactions and additions at a distance.

Vision: suggests a future-oriented, creative, or persuasive perspective that, when shared, can inspire collective efforts to achieve a common goal; an attractive vision of future directions for lifelong learning can be an important feature of shared leadership by educators of adults in each stakeholder role.

Vocation: a commitment to important values and benefits that may or may not coincide with an occupation that may change a number of times during an adult's work life; a related meaning of vocational education emphasizes skill performance in working-class occupations.

Voluntary: along with volunteer work, contributions in associations, enterprises, and organizations entail adults choosing to use their time and abilities for that purpose, rather than as a requirement for paid work.

Webinar: a seminar experience that can be provided for participants electronically with use of computer technology and related communications.

Well-Being: a general concept about components of quality of life such as health, prosperity, and happiness.

Wellness: emphasizes prevention and avoiding illness and poor health.

Wisdom: a perspective on people and society that emphasizes insight, use of accumulated philosophical and scientific knowledge, discernment of inner qualities and relationships, sound judgment, importance of values, and consideration of potential results and by-products from alternative courses of action.

Women: adult females.

Work: accomplishing beneficial and productive tasks as a volunteer, or as a source of income, which is characteristic of work in a family, enterprise, or association.

Workplace: an arrangement and location for work and employment, which, with technology and some occupations, may occur at remote or varied locations.

Workshop: a method of teaching and learning in which adult participants and the people who help them engage in planning, conducting, and evaluating the activity.

Written: referring to communication and use of text-based language, it is a potential participant proficiency, in contrast to dependence on oral communication, which is a major influence on various ways of initiating and sustaining participation by some adults and basic education; regarding occupation and communication, also includes participation by adults who may be literate but depend mainly on oral communication.

APPENDIX

Contents for Volume Two, Volume Three, and Volume Four

Volume Two

Volume Three

Volume Four

EDITORS AND CONTRIBUTORS

Core Editors

Simone C.O. Conceição, PhD, is a professor and chair in the Department of Administrative Leadership at the University of Wisconsin–Milwaukee. She received her doctorate in adult and distance education from the University of Wisconsin–Madison and her master's in adult and continuing education leadership from the University of Wisconsin–Milwaukee. She has served on the editorial board of six journals; published numerous articles in peer-reviewed journals; written more than 20 book chapters; and authored five books on the topics of online education, adult learning, online student motivation and support, and faculty workload when teaching online.

Alan B. Knox is professor emeritus in educational leadership at the University of Wisconsin–Madison. He recently served for two years as one of three coeditors of this international compendium. His teaching, writing, speaking, editing, and administrative work have all gradually evolved since he began work in the field in 1946. Inducted into the International Adult and Continuing Education Hall of Fame in 1996, he is a past president of the American Association for Adult and Continuing Education (AAACE) and has chaired national commissions on adult education. He has received the Okes Award for Outstanding Research in Adult Education twice and is the author of many publications, including *Evaluation for Continuing Education: A Comprehensive Guide to Success* (Jossey-Bass, 2002), which won the Houle Award for Outstanding Literature in Adult Education in 2003.

Larry G. Martin is professor emeritus of adult and continuing education leadership at the University of Wisconsin–Milwaukee. As a faculty member for more than 36 years, he routinely taught graduate courses on program planning in adult education, administration of adult education programs, evaluation of adult education programs, and others. For 20 years he served in a number of administrative roles in higher education. A 2015 inductee into the International Adult and Continuing Education Hall of Fame, he has published three edited books and numerous articles and book chapters. He earned a PhD at the University of Wisconsin–Madison.

Consulting Editors

Lisa M. Baumgartner, PhD, is an associate professor of adult education at Texas A&M University. Her research includes adult learning and development in marginalized populations and issues of diversity.

Michelle Glowacki-Dudka, PhD, is an associate professor of adult, higher, and community education in the Department of Educational Studies, Teachers College, at Ball State University, Muncie, Indiana.

Allan Quigley was professor of adult education at St. Francis Xavier University, Nova Scotia, and associate professor at Pennsylvania State University. His career includes government service as well as college-level teaching and administration in both the United States and Canada.

Mark Tennant is an emeritus professor of education at the University of Technology, Sydney. Tennant has published widely and has been the recipient of the Cyril O. Houle Award for Literature in adult education.

Editorial Coordinator

Anita Samuel, PhD, is an educational teaching and research associate at the Uniformed Services University of Health Sciences. She also lectures in the Department of Administrative Leadership at the University of Wisconsin–Milwaukee. Her research interests are online learning and faculty development.

Contributors

Emily Auerbach is a professor of English and director of the UW Odyssey Project at the University of Wisconsin–Madison. She is also cohost of University of the Air, a program on Wisconsin Public Radio.

Wei-Wen Chang is professor of international human resource development at National Taiwan Normal University. She received her PhD from the

University of Wisconsin–Madison. Her research focuses on learning psychology and intercultural competence development.

Patricia Cranton, PhD, (deceased) was a leading adult educator whose publications surrounding adult learning have influenced generations of scholars not only in North America but also internationally.

Ankur R. Desai is a professor of atmospheric and oceanic sciences, faculty affiliate, at Nelson Institute Center for Climatic Research at the University of Wisconsin–Madison.

Brian Findsen, professor, teaches adult education in the Faculty of Education at the University of Waikato in New Zealand. He has worked in the field of adult and continuing education for more than 30 years in New Zealand and Glasgow, Scotland.

Mahlet Gebremariam is a consultant and assistant professor in obstetrics and gynecology in the Department of Obstetrics and Gynecology, College of Health Sciences, at Addis Ababa University in Addis Ababa, Ethiopia.

Cynthia Haq is professor of family medicine and community health at the University of Wisconsin School of Medicine and Public Health. She is a champion for health equity, primary health care, and community health.

Doe Hentschel, PhD, is vice president of Leadership Greater Hartford in Hartford, Connecticut.

Alejandro R. Jadad is a physician, educator, researcher, innovator, and entrepreneur whose mission is to enable all people to live full, healthy, and happy lives, in love, until their last breath, as part of a flourishing planet.

Tamen Jadad-Garcia is an international entrepreneur and innovator. Her ventures focus on the creation and spread of health, the understanding and cultivation of love, and the promotion of human flourishing through the entire life cycle.

Robert Jecklin, MPH, PhD, is most interested in informal learning related to aging, health care, population health, and travel. He currently works at the University of Wisconsin–La Crosse.

Sarah Korpi, PhD, is the academic program director for independent learning in the Division of Continuing Studies at the University of Wisconsin–Madison.

Elizabeth Kvach, MD, MA, is a full-time family physician with Denver Health and an assistant professor of family medicine with the University of Colorado–Denver's Family Medicine Residency Program in Denver.

Sandra L. Morrison is associate professor at the University of Waikato in Hamilton, New Zealand. Morrison is an indigenous Māori woman from Te Arawa, Tainui, and Maniapoto tribes.

Andrea Nikischer is an assistant professor in the adult education department at SUNY Buffalo State. She previously worked as a sexual assault prevention educator and activist. Nikischer has a PhD in educational culture, policy, and society.

Edward R. Purse is a senior learning adviser for the government of Canada and a PhD candidate at the University of Ottawa, Faculty of Education, Canada. His research interests include workplace and transformative learning.

Carol Rogers-Shaw is a PhD candidate in adult education at Pennsylvania State University. Her research interests include universal design for learning, increasing access to higher education and lifelong learning, and identity development of learners with disabilities.

M. Cecil Smith, PhD, is associate dean for research and graduate education and professor of learning sciences and human development at West Virginia University. His research focuses on adults' literacy practices and proficiencies.

Fiker Taddesse is an assistant professor of pharmacology and department head of pharmacology at Awassa University in Awassa, Ethiopia.

Edward W. Taylor is a professor of lifelong learning and adult education at Pennsylvania State University–Harrisburg.

Maurice C. Taylor is a professor in the faculty of education and chair in university teaching at the University of Ottawa, Canada, where he teaches and supervises in the domain of adult education.

David L. Trumpower is an associate professor in the faculty of education at the University of Ottawa, Canada. His research interests involve statistics education, adult learning, and the development of educational assessment instruments.

Timote Vaioleti is a researcher with the University of Waikato, Hamilton, New Zealand. Vaioleti is from the Pacific nation of Tonga.

INDEX

Bolded page numbers refer to glossary definitions.

The American Association for Adult and Continuing Education (AAACE) is a professional association providing leadership for the field of adult, community and continuing education through publications, conferences, advocacy, and dissemination of research and best practices. AAACE was founded in 1982.

The mission of AAACE is to provide leadership for the field of adult and continuing education by expanding opportunities for adult growth and development; unifying adult educators; fostering the development and dissemination of theory, research, information, and best practices; promoting identity and standards for the profession; and advocating relevant public policy and social change initiatives. AAACE is dedicated to the belief that lifelong learning contributes to human fulfillment and positive social change. AAACE members envision a more humane world made possible by the diverse practice of the members in helping adults acquire the knowledge, skills and values needed to lead productive and satisfying lives. AAACE publishes the leading adult education journals in the field: Adult Education Quarterly (AEQ), Adult Learning (AL), and the Journal of Transformative Education (JTED). In addition, the organization publishes the Handbook of Adult and Continuing Education every 10 years. The AAACE annual conference is held in different regions of the country on a rotating basis, often in partnership with state, regional, or other national and international associations. Several AAACE commissions offer pre-conferences and co-conferences during the annual conference, including the Commission on International Adult Education, the Commission of Professors of Adult Education, the Commission for Distance Learning and Technology.

Visit www.aaace.org for more information on AAACE.